THE GOLD GUIDES

CAPRI

EB BONECHI

© Copyright by Casa Editrice Bonechi - Via dei Cairoli 18b - Firenze - Italia
Phone + 39 055 576841 - Fax + 39 055 5000766
E-mail: bonechi@bonechi.it - Internet: www.bonechi.it

Publication created and designed by: Casa Editrice Bonechi
Graphic design and picture research: Serena de Leonardis
Video pagemaking and cover: Bernardo Dionisio
Texts by Giuliano Valdes (Editing Studio, Pisa) and Patrizia Fabbri in collaboration with the
Editorial Department of Casa Editrice Bonechi.
The drawing on page 56 is by Stefano Benini.
Translation by Rhiannon Lewis.

Printed in Italy by Centro Stampa Editoriale Bonechi

PICTURE CREDITS:

The majority of the photographs are property of Casa Editrice Bonechi and were taken by
Paolo Giambone;
p. 67 bottom, Foto Amendola; pp. 4, 7, 8, 9, 10 center right, 22, 24, 28 bottom,
32, 33, 57, 61 bottom and top right, 66--67, 78, Foto Farella.
The photographs relative to the recipes are property of Casa Editrice Bonechi
and were taken by Andrea Alteri, Andrea Fantauzzo, Aldo Settembre, and Franco Tomasello.

Other photographs were supplied by the archives listed below:
Foto Atlantide/Stefano Amantini: pp.10 bottom, 18, 46, 92.
Foto Gaetano Barone: pp. 16, 67. Foto Andrea Innocenti: pp. 11, 12, 13, 14, 15, 20 left.
The photographs at the top of page 20 are used with the kind permission of Umberto Pollio.

Every effort has been made to trace the copyright holders and we apologize in advance for
any unintentional omissions. We woulde pleased to include the appropriate
acknowledgments in any future edition.

ISBN 88-476-0785-X

* * *

The Isle of Capri, the "Pearl of the Mediterranean," in a suggestive view from the Sorrento peninsula.

INTRODUCTION

In the everchanging and vast panorama of the minor islands of Italy, Capri holds a position of absolute privilege. If on the one hand every island has well-defined characteristics and special particularities which help to give a tourist image, on the other hand the very mention of Capri — evokes an inextricable mixture of sensations which exalt the dimensions of a Mediterranean island par excellence.

Capri is essentially a fairy tale, a dream lost in the extra-ordinary azure of an incredible sea, in the boundless panoramas which embrace other precious tesserae of that wonderful mosaic which is the Neapolitan and Salerno coast, between Capo Miseno and Amalfi.

Everything which can be perceived by the senses finds its greatest elevation on this island; from the light, sublime complement and refined facets of colour which allow one to read, as in an open book, the endless wonders of the place; from the perfume of the flowers which constitute another jewel of the island and the vegetation which is a mixture of Mediterranean aspects and more precisely tropical ones: from the strong salt-laden breezes of a sea which is the very life of the island; from the disturbing voice of silence, broken only by the piercing cry of the seagulls and the breaking of the waves on the steep and precipitous rocks; from the possibility of touching with one's own hands the ancient traces of an illustrious and fascinating history, together with numerous remains of a past which represents the most authentic cultural metrix of the place; from the rough, yet sublime taste of the refined cuisine of Capri, to the rich taste of its noble wines produced on rough but generous land.

3

GEOGRAPHICAL PROFILE - The island which is frequently linked to the mainland (Naples and Sorrento) by boats and hovercraft is only 5 kms from Punta Campanella, which represents the furthermost point of the Sorrento peninsular. Its polulation (12.500 approx.) is spread out over the two Communes of Capri and Anacapri. The total surface area is around 11 square kms and measures approximately 6 kms in length and at its widest point measures around 3 kms. The circumference of its coasts measures 17 kms.

In the most remote geological era Capri was definitely part of the morphological and structural unity of the Sorrent peninsular, from which it was later separated due to the major techtonic and orogenetic upheavals. Unlike the Flegree islands which are situated in front of the Campi Flegree in the upper portion of the wide Neapolitan gulf, Capri does not have vulcanic origins.

The island is set in front of the Sorrento peninsular, from which it is separated by a narrow strait of water called Bocca Piccola. The geological structure of Capri is prevalently calcarea with the presence of tuff and pozzuolana transported by the winds during the paroxysmal vulcanic eruptions of Campi Flegree and Vesuvius. The coasts which are high and rocky offer a large number of grottoes and are surrounded by rocks which rise out of the water, such as the famous Faraglioni. The highest mountains are Mount Solaro (589 m) the Mount St. Maria (499 m) and Mount Tiberius (335 m).

Capri has very few rivers (although there are a few small transitory streams in the westernmost area) and because of the complete lack of springs a plant for extracting salt from sea water has recently been installed so as to provide the drinking water necessary for the population and for the numerous tourists. The flora of Capri has characteristcs which are similar to that of the Sorrento peninsular and has a decidedly Mediterranean aspect including the presence of well over 850 species and 133 varieties. The fauna of the island consists mainly of seagulls even though rare animals such as the sea-cow (Monachus monachus) are to be found although unfortunately they are becoming extinct. Also to be found is the singular *Lacerta coerulea faraglionensis* commonly known as the blue lizard.

The characteristics of the climate of Capri are typical of a Mediterranean island and therefore result in numerous mild days throughout the year. Even in summer the temperatures are generally under 30° and this is thanks to the moderate yet constant sea breezes which, as well as having a thermo-regulator function, keep the island free from damp sea mists, exalting the spectacular island scenery accentuated by an intensely clear blue sky. In winter the temperatures are, on the whole, quite pleasant, with a complete absence of frost.

The economic structure of Capri is largely based on tourism which, in the last decades, has enjoyed a boom. Probably Capri's reputation as a tourist Mecca dates back to the last century when it was discovered by the Swedish writer and doctor Axel Munthe and was visited by such illustrious names as Ferdinand Gregorovius, Alexandre Dumas, August von Platen-Hallermünde and others. In more recent times Maxim Gorki, Curzio Malaparte and Ada Negri consolidated and perpetuated the tradition of the island as a paradise for meditation and inspiration. A refined first-class hotel structure, a high level of recreational structures and its fame as a seaside resort all contribute in making Capri a Mecca of international tourism. Another important aspect of the island's economy is the fishing industry and the handicraft industry — which produces beautiful ceramics and majolica, coral jewellery, hand-made baskets and large wicker baskets, and espadrilles — important crops (vines and olive groves), citrus fruits, together with other cottage industries (textiles and woodwork).

HISTORY - Of the many versions given for the origin of the place-name — *Caprea* according to Strabone, to indicate the harsh conformation of its rocky soil, or *Capraim* which comes from a semitic expression which means "two villages" — *Capreae* is without doubt the more convincing because it would refer as Varone ascertaines, to the considerable presence of wild boars on the island (*Caprios* according to Greek spelling). The fact that Capri was a Greek colony is now certain even if it is believed that it was populated as far back as the palaeolithic age, during the period of major vulcanic activity in the Flegrea regions, when the island formed part of the mainland. This latter ascertion is

Clear, deep waters bathe the wild, rocky coasts of Capri.

The Faraglioni "framed" by a typical Mediterranean pine.

backed by the extraordinary archeological discoveries which date back to Roman times, when, during the building of monumental villas, the bones of prehistoric animals and stone weapons were found. At the beginning of this century, during excavation work for the foundations of the Quisisana Hotel other prehistoric weapons and the bones of animals such as the *Rhinoceros Merckii,* the *Ursus spelaeus* and the *Elephas primigenius* were found. If the Greek presence on Capri can be proved by the numerous greek epigraphs and by the existence, during the Roman Imperial Age of a greek term used to describe the appointing of municipal magistrates (*agoranómi*), the presence of the Phoenicians who seem to have established the commercial landing places on the island has yet to be proved. The Roman "discovery" of Capri dates back to 29 A.D. when Augustus landed here on his way back to Rome after the Eastern campagns. Having fallen in love with the island, he took it from the Neapolitans, giving them Ischia in return. His presence marks a transformation in the juridicial and administrative aspects of the island, which from this date would undergo radical changes due to the building work done on the island such as the construction of sumptuous villas and splendid residences.

After the death of Augustus (14 A.D.) his successor Tiberius, made Capri his "golden exile", choosing the island as his home for the last decade of his life. The chronicles of Tacito and Svetonio give a dark and gloomy portrait of Tiberius underlining the most perverse and evil aspects of his character, without paying hommage to the notable qualities of the man, which a more objective and indirect historiographical judgement would surely give. His death (37 A.D.) which took place near the Villa of Lucullo at Miseo, whilst he was trying to reach his beloved island, marked the beginning of the decline of Capri together with the changing attitude of the Romans towards the island, who, apart from a few exceptions, would, from this point onwards, use it as an exile for people who created trouble in the capital.

Such was the destiny of Lucilla and Crispina, respectively the sister and the mother of the Emperor Commodo (182 A.D.).

At the fall of the Roman Empire Capri was controlled by the abbots of Montecasino and by Neapolitans, and was subjected to frequent pirate raids especially those of the Saracens. Then it was controlled by the Longobards who were followed by the Normans and then the island passed from one domination to another including the Aragonesi, Angioini, and the raids of the Turkish pirates Khair ad-Din (*Barbarossa*) and Dragut. For a long time it came under Spanish administration and suffered a great plague (18th century), and then finally it was governed by the Borbons. It was contended by the French and English at the time of the Napoleonic Wars, after which it was ruled once more by the Borbons of Naples before its annexation to the newly formed Kingdom of Italy thereby establishing the characteristics which it now maintains as one of the obligatory stages of international tourism.

HOLIDAYS AND TRADITIONS

THE TARANTELLA

It is not known for certain whether this dance is named after the city of Taranto or the tarantula, as it is said that it has therapeutic properties against the latter's bite, which can cause violent convulsions. It is, however, certain that the tarantella is still one of the most typical and well-loved dances of the Campania region, where it became particularly popular from the XVIIIth century onwards. Danced in couples, with the accompaniment of tambourines, accordions, other peculiar classical instruments and, sometimes, singing, the tarantella is characterised by a marked rhythm which gradually gathers pace: after a relatively slow start, it reaches heights of authentic paroxysm.

HOLIDAYS AND TRADITIONS

THE PATRON SAINT

For centuries, the rivalry dividing the two main municipalities of the island was also embodied in the confrontation between two different patron saints, Saint
Costanzo for Capri and Saint Anthony for Anacapri. The feast of Saint Costanzo,
with its fascinating repetition of rites and traditions, is celebrated on May 14th. A
procession leaves the church dedicated to the saint, not far from Aiano, and
moves down towards the marina for the blessing of the sea, and then returns to
the church for a solemn commemoration of Saint Costanzo's arrival on the island, an event which, according to ecclesiastic tradition, occurred around 739.
Venerated relics remain as evidence of the times when Capri had a primitive
house belonging to the Order of Saint Basil and a convent in the inland hills, destined for centuries to provide a safe refuge for the population from raids and the
much-feared incursions of the Saracen pirates.

HOLIDAYS AND TRADITIONS

GOOD FRIDAY

One of the most famous traditions, deeply rooted in the heart of Capri's population, is undoubtedly the one linked to the Good Friday liturgy, with solemn mourning at the statue depicting the dead Christ, whose tortured body is covered in sores and wounds, and the procession, in which large numbers of people always participate. The great popular devotion, the presence of the religious authorities, and the absolute respect of precise rituals handed down over the centuries give Good Fridays on the island an aura of enthralling sacredness.

THE FORMS AND SHAPES OF CAPRI

The island of Capri rises from the extreme depths of the so-called Terrace-Bridge of Salerno in front of Bocca Piccola, which separates it from the Sorrento peninsula. The strange forms created by erosion, the Faraglioni, and the sheer cliffs bring to mind the Dolomites. And in fact, geological study of the subsoil of Capri reveals calcareous materials of Cretaceous and Eocene origin, while the tufa and pozzolana are the results of processes of wind-borne deposit and sedimentation during the episodes of violent volcanic activity of nearby Vesuvius and the Phlegraean area in general.

The harsh coasts of the island arouse

intense emotions, which are mitigated by views of landscapes and towns of indescribable beauty. The coasts are prevalently high, rocky, and difficult to reach. There are many natural caves and grottoes, which together with the many free-standing rocks (including the famous Faraglioni), only exalt the sinuous and multifaceted aspect of the coastline. The most famous of the grottoes, the Grotta Azzurra, provides proof that a latent yet unrelenting bradyseismic phenomenon, which has already lowered the grotto itself and of the Baths of Tiberius, is still occurring.

From the morphological point of view, Capri is formed of two plateaus separated by a narrow saddle along which lies the town of Capri, the administrative center of the island. The highland in the eastern portion of the island slopes gently up to the 335-meters' elevation of Monte Tiberio; the western and larger plateau is steeper, rising to 589 meters at Monte Solaro, the island's highest peak.

Another recurring theme in the landscapes of Capri is the Sorrento peninsula, which stands out in the backgrounds of the most famous views of the island and which, on a clear day, seems almost near enough reach out and touch. In very remote geological eras, this morphological feature of mainland Campania was joined to Capri, which at the time constituted a promontory advancing into the Tyrhennian Sea. Later massive tectonic movements later separated it from the peninsula and moved it out into the sea as an island.

THE ISLAND PLANTS AND PERFUMES

One of the environmental features most characteristic of the whole of this splendid Tyrhennian island is the profusion of flowers, plants, and flora in general that lend it its truly unforgettable aspect. In spite of its harsh morphology, Capri is an essentially "green" island. Besides growing exuberantly the parks, in the gardens and orchards, on the terraces and balconies (and, in fact, wherever man has decided to embellish his own works, flowers also stubbornly colonize all kinds of terrain, including the most inaccessible and impervious rocky gorges. These splashes of color, which in the most favorable season, under a clear blue sky, exalt the innate lyricism of the island landscape and perhaps represent its most inviting "calling card," are the subject of admired contemplation by tourists and travelers. Beyond the classical cloak of vegetation that mantles the slopes of the island, the higher elevations host evergreen scrub formations.

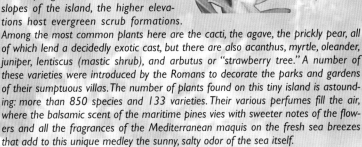

Among the most common plants here are the cacti, the agave, the prickly pear, all of which lend a decidedly exotic cast, but there are also acanthus, myrtle, oleander, juniper, lentiscus (mastic shrub), and arbutus or "strawberry tree." A number of these varieties were introduced by the Romans to decorate the parks and gardens of their sumptuous villas. The number of plants found on this tiny island is astounding: more than 850 species and 133 varieties. Their various perfumes fill the air, where the balsamic scent of the maritime pines vies with sweeter notes of the flowers and all the fragrances of the Mediterranean maquis on the fresh sea breezes that add to this unique medley the sunny, salty odor of the sea itself.

The white flowers and tiny fruits of Myrtus communis, an evergreen shrub; above, a detail of a member of the family Euphorbiaceae. Both plants, typical of the Mediterranean area, often play important roles in the myths and legends of the peoples of this region.

A Botanical Eden

Capri's reputation as an earthly Garden of Eden is well deserved, since in a little less than 10 square kilometers it hosts, as we have already said, a great many species and varieties of flora. Autochthonous plants grow alongside the exotic species introduced to beautify the gardens (and by now spontaneous island plants) and some true rarities, like the dwarf fan palm (Chamaerops humilis – facing page, bottom – found only on the northwestern coast of the island between the Grotta Azzurra and the Baths of Tiberius) that together with the fossil remains of many vertebrates show how millions of years ago Capri was connected to the Sorrento peninsula, with its subtropical climate

favorable to this type of plant.
When the Romans came to Capri, they found an island dominated by high Mediterranean maquis, with evergreen oak forests that with the passing of time have disappeared to make space for man's activities. The Romans brought their own plants, like the "Taraentina" variety of myrtle, which by now are well integrated in the ecosystem of the island.

On these pages are just some examples of Capri's flora. From left to right and top to bottom, the agave, of Mexican origin but by now naturalized in many places throughout the Mediterranean area, with its lanceolate leaves and tall inflorescence (which can reach 12 meters); two images of rosemary, an evergreen shrub typical of the Mediterranean maquis, with tiny light

blue to purplish flowers that effuse an inebriating fragrance during the hot days; an euphorbia bush on the beach – this plant, like the mastic shrub that dots the coastal cliffs, prefers sunny places.

The Monte Barbarossa Oasis

Capri's flora, so lush and varied, with many autochthonous species and exotic plants introduced over time, is surely one of the major tourist attractions of the island — but no less so is its fauna. The deep waters surrounding the island are inhabited by many marine species, and the wide array of terrestrial fauna includes even a rare lizard, the Lacerta coerulea muralis or "faraglionensis" – described for the first time by the famous physician and paleontologist Ignazio Cerio, father of the just as well known Edwin – with its peculiar bluish coloring. This lizard was once thought to live only on the Faraglioni of Capri, but now seems to be found in Sicily as well.

The Oasis managed by WWF Italia on Monte Barbarossa, in the town of Anacapri, was founded in 1997. The area, which may be visited from May through September, covers 6 hectares and is part of the huge park owned by the Swedish Axel Munthe Foundation.

It is characterized by its garrigues, typical Mediterranean brush formations with low evergreen plants like thyme, rosemary, and other plants typical of only a few areas of the island, such as the cytisus, a flowering shrub similar to the broom. Pearl grass and hyssop, with their blue and violet flowers, red valerian, and the anemones, the euphorbias, and the orchids all lend notes of color to the lush

Above, an Euphorbia peplis; *below, two thickets of* Euphorbia dendroides. *Right, a peregrine falcon, the symbol of the Oasis.*

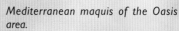

Mediterranean maquis of the Oasis area.

Obviously, this is the ideal habitat for many insects, like the Cetonia aurata or goldsmith beetle, and such butterflies as the beautiful swallow-tail, with its broad yellow wings.

Many small mammals also inhabit the area. The Oasis is known for its scientific work with avifauna, and in fact hosts a ringing station for migratory birds. The symbol of the Oasis is the peregrine falcon, which nests on the island. This bird of prey, with a wingspan known to exceed one meter and capable of dizzying plunges to make a catch, prefers high trees and rocky cliffs – of which there are so many on Capri – for building its nest.

Above, the inflorescence of Rosmarinus officinalis*; below, an* Orchis italica *and an flower of the* Anemone coronaria*; right,* Acanthus mollis.

MARINA GRANDE

It is difficult for a person who does not know Capri to imagine the emotions and the surprise of the tourist or traveller who sets foot on this enchanted island for the first time. Marina Grande, as is quite clear from its name, is the main port and the most frequented landing place of the island as well as a colourful and fascinating introduction to the picturesque and suggestive microcosm of Capri.

Here, in the Augustian age there was a sandy shore, the *Grande Marina* which the Romans used as a landing place for their ships and which afterwards became a port, situated in a more easterly location than the present infrastructure in harmony with *Punta Vivara*, from where one reached the imperial residence of **Palazzo a Mare**. The traces of this ancient maritime landing place, fortified and reinforced by Tiberius who wanted to facilitate communications between it and the fleet which was quartered in the roadstead of Misseno can still be seen today and give testimony of the important role of the island in the most splendid era of the Roman Empire, between the first century B.C. and the first century A.D.

Today Marina Grande is a beautiful riverside town which is set in a lovely natural position at the foot of the green saddle along which the romantic town of Capri stretches. The town of Marina Grande has merged with the above lying main town; in the small square which overlooks the port and which is usually swarming with tourists, stand, the characteristic houses of Capri, rendered typical by the terraces, by the balconies, by the open galleries and by the multicoloured facades of the town, brightened by the "Pompeian red" which is one of the most intense notes of colour along the whole Neapolitan coast.

Two views of the picturesque village of Marina Grande, set on a broad bay opening on the Gulf of Naples. The island's major port, Marina Grande has been used as a harbor since the Roman era.

The first sensations felt by the tourist, the first contact with this unique island, are of a fairytale nature: one's gaze, which is at first drawn to the picturesque port, to the boats and to the sequence of enchanting houses, is then directed to the green slopes which dominate Marina and which allow one to catch a glimpse of the first few houses of Capri, on the summit of the saddle. Amidst the steep terraced slopes, covered with an exuberant and blooming Mediterranean flora, or otherwise covered with vines, stand out the marvellous foilage of the maritime pines, whilst the white houses scenically set out in the shape of an amphitheatre on the background of the steep crags of calcareous rocks all contribute to form a part of this wonderful Mediterranean crib.

Each end of the port of Marina Grande has two imposing wharfs at the end of the western wharf there is a *Coloumn* with a corinthian capital, placed on a high pedestal and this is proof of the important significance (even felt today) of the Roman presence on Capri. In the eastern part of the port a modern, well-equipped tourist dock is used by the sailors and by the beautiful boats which help to underline the tourist "enigma" and worldwide fame of this dream island.

However the most "vivid" aspect of Marina Grande is the large number of fishing boats, moored along the waters of the shore line or beached along the shore. Here, in front of the houses (which were once used as warehouses) the fishermen of the island carry out their work, either mending their multicoloured boats or repairing their nets while they wait for the most favourable moment to set sail.

During the tourist season, one can see, on the western wharf the coming and going of boats and hovercrafts which provide the connections between the mainland and the island, and numerous boats, motorboats and all types of craft set sail crowded with tourists to carry out the round trip of the island. The boat trip around the island, like the visits to the numerous **Grottoes** and to the **Faraglioni** can only be carried out when weather conditions, the sea and the tides permit.

Another lovely image of the port of Marina Grande, with its vivid colors.
Facing page, the entrance to the funicular that links the town of Capri and Marina Grande. The cable railway runs above cultivated slopes and homes that seem to cling to the overhanging rock.

THE FUNICULAR

This singular means of transportation leaps immediately to the tourist's eye. Despite the fact that a modern panoramic road permits the taxis and Capri's public transportation system (during the high season, non-residents are strictly prohibited from bringing their cars to the island) to reach the town, thousands of tourists and visitors choose the picturesque little cable railway train that climbs directly from Marina Grande to Capri. Apropos of the funicular, Fiorella Romana recounts in "Capri" (La Campania paese per paese, Bonechi Editore, 1999) how "the funicular, with its two open-windowed cars of a beautiful brilliant red, was inaugurated a little before the 1906 visit of the German emperor William II. In truth, the debut of the new means of transportation was not felicitous – during one of the very first trips two of the cables broke, causing the destruction of one of the cars and the death of two passengers. Luckily, the islanders' pride and the charm of the train, so attractive to the tourists who in the early 1900s began to visit the island, very soon dispelled the negative effect produced by the sad event, and before long the funicular was enjoying the success it merited."

The route of the funicular winds up the shady terraced slopes that from the saddle on which the town is set decline steeply to the port. This unusual and probably a bit outdated means of transportation is entertaining and certainly in harmony with the basically harsh natural structure of the island. The steep rocky peaks seen from the windows of the train loom over the characteristic small homes and buildings scattered along the sides of the mountain, all terraces and porticoes facing the sea, in the midst of fields and vineyards alternating with luxuriant evergreen Mediterranean macchia.

CURIOSITIES OF CAPRI

Miniature Capri

All the charm of the places, historic moments, and customs in a small yet large work of art. The pride of Anacapri. An elegant jewel created by the expert hands of maestro Sergio Rubino, a famous Capri ceramist. An interesting itinerary provides details of the main places on the island through the use of grey and blue limestone and ceramics. To make the setting more natural, dwarf specimens of the island's typical vegetation have been used and the work is surrounded by water, an essential and congenial element. The reproduction of the island measures twenty by ten meters and recalls Capri's historic, archaeological and naturalistic spirit. The Faraglioni, the Grotta Azzurra, crossed by the typical rowboat, the

red funicular railway, and the characteristic chair lift are all faithfully reproduced. The famous "Piazzetta" has the same blue and yellow bell-tower. The work is surrounded by eleven showcases with allegoric representations of the main scenes of life on Capri: from the Roman empire to the discovery of the Grotta Azzurra (1826).
Adjacent to "Miniature Capri" is an interesting ceramics gallery which, in addition to illustrating ceramic production with the use of a typical kiln, invites visitors to attend a lesson on the use of ceramics and the various stage in its manufacture.

An Air of Capri

The crafts tradition on Capri does not stop at production of ceramics or the traditional rope sandals, decorated with many special materials, of which so many movie stars and celebrities have become enamored. It continues on to production of perfumes – perfumes unique in the world. But on an island where so many fragrances fill the air, released by such a singular collection of plants and flowers as is Capri's, it is perhaps only natural that those who have the good fortune to breathe them should succumb to the desire to capture and imprison them in glass bottles. It would seem that Capri's perfume-making tradition originated centuries ago at the Certosa di San Giacomo. A chemist from the Piemonte region, while conducting research in the archives of the monastery, came upon some ancient formulas for distilling perfumed essences (formulas created, it is thought, by the father prior of San Giacomo following the visit of the queen of Naples, Jeanne d'Anjou, to Capri. From the will to perpetuate the perfume making tradition there was born a laboratory that produces, with the essences of lemon, orange, peach, and mimosa, an ancient fragrance known for its exquisite delicacy. Due to its success, the laboratory has increased the scope of its production and today also offers a wide range of scents for men, in which rosemary predominates, and for women, in some of which the essences of as many as 25 flowers are concentrated.

CAPRI

This is the main town and the major centre of the island and stretches along the saddleback which lies between Mount St. Maria, Mount Tuoro and Mount Tiberius. Due to the spectacular beauty of its natural position (inserted in a geographical context of marvellous landscapes) Capri is considered to be one of the "pearls" of world tourism, the main goal of the tourists who visit the "minor islands", as well as being a place which is visited by tourists who come from all over the world.

The irresistible fascination of this extraordinary town is rendered above all by the salient traits of the towns and houses of Capri, which mirror the Mediterranean forms of architecture, such as the unending sequences of white houses which are all the more enchanting because of their terraces and loggias. A secondary characteristic element is the topographical order of the town, which is a picturesque labyrinth of streets and alleys which are often alternated or crossed by narrow lanes, surmounted by arches and arcades-clear proof of the ancient Medieval plan of the town.

The *piazza Umberto 1* is universally known as the "**Piazzetta**": it is the throbbing heart of the main town as well as being the main tourist attraction of the island. Once known as the "little theatre of the world" it is really the "drawing

The panorama from the belvedere of Capri is one of unequaled beauty and suggestion.

Another image from the belvedere of Capri. Facing page, the Torre dell'Orologio dominates Piazza Umberto I, "La Piazzetta" par excellence, since time immemorial the center of tourist and society life in the island's major town.

room" of Capri; at the tables of the cafès, which are shaded by multicoloured and characteristic umbrellas, the most important and prestigious people from the world of the cinema, fashion, literature, and politics and the composite world of business have sat.

It is an important meeting point and an obligatory stop for the crowds of tourists who come here throughout the whole year. The small piazza opens out on the site of where the first Greek colonies established the acropolis, between the V and the IV centuries B.C.. Imposing traces of the ancient tombs of Capri, built in the Greek period are still visible near the mountain cablecar station, inserted amongst the houses and the town perimetry which has a Medieval plan. The small piazza is dominated by the **Clocktower**, once the belltower of the ancient cathedral, and has a small cupola which has a decidedly eastern stamp, under which small arcades which house the bells open out. At one end of this charming centre lies the **Town Hall**, once the residence of the Bishop, which has a facade covered with plaques, whilst opposite this building stands the animated facade of the **Church of St. Stephen** which can be reached by a small flight of steps.

Beyond the Clocktower, the piazza opens out onto the small loggia of *Belvedere*, characterized by a succession of white coloumns placed on high pedestals. From the parapet of the small loggia one can admire one of the most spectacular views of the whole island, which stretches out from the unmistakable profile of Ischia to the Flegrea region and the whole Neapolitan gulf, dominated by the menacing outline of Vesuvius. The view is particularly enchanting in the late evening when the numerous lights of Capri are seen against the dark profile of the mountains, softened by the twilight, and making an enchanting fairylike picture which is almost like a Christmas crib.

TAKE THE OLD TAXI

Since non-residents are strictly prohibited from using private cars on the island for about seven months a year, the visitor must go by public transport or take the occasion to make his trip even more pleasurable by taking the characteristic taxis of Capri. These picturesque means of transport will shuttle you all over the island on the modern panoramic road as well as through the town on its charming narrow streets. What is so "picturesque" about a taxi? On Capri, they are all antique automobiles, true connoisseur's jewels, and usually quite large. They have all been adapted for public use: some of the vehicles have even been lengthened, to carry up to seven passengers.

The taxis are one of the myriad attractions of Capri that cannot escape the visitor's attention — in part due to the gaudy colors that distinguish these automobiles, which are now by now an integral part of the scenario of the island.

The facade of the church of Santo Stefano, designed in the late 17th century.

THE CHURCH OF ST. STEPHEN - This place of worship acts as a frame for one of the most characteristic views of the picturesque small piazza. The building which we see today is the result of a late 17th century project presided over by the architect Picchiatti and brought to completion by Marziale Desiderio of Amalfi who gave the typical forms of the architecture of Capri a decidedly Baroque characteristic. The exterior of the building (which stands on the site of a primitive cathedral, of which only the *Clocktower* remains) is characterized by its facade, enlivened by the curvilinear architecture upon which are inserted some tambours, these being surmounted by beautiful eastern-style cupolas. The building is dominated by a central dome, opened at the base by a series of arched windows. The facade, consisting of two orders, has a decidedly Baroque aspect, as can be seen by the curvilinear trend of the upper order, enriched by ornamental motifs. The upper order, vertically scanned by pilaster strips has two large niches containing statues. The most important artistic element that one can admire inside the church is the floor under the main altar: this is of a series of colourful pieces brought here from the *Villa Jovis*, the most celebrated of the many villas of Tiberius. In the *Chapel of the Rosary* some fragments of another Roman floor have been set out, which, in all probability was transfered from another Roman residence: the *Villa of Tragara*. Amongst the other works of artistic interest, the funeral monuments of the Arcucci should be noted. These were carried out by the Florentine sculptor Michelangelo Naccherino (16-17th century), and also a picture dating back to the XVIth century depicting the *Madonna with Child and Saints Michael and Anthony*. This painting is the object of particular devotion amongst the people of Capri, because legend has is that it played a part in a miracle which is thought to have taken place during the time of the pirate raids on the island.

PALAZZO CERIO - The bulding is situated at the extreme end of a piazza which bears the same name, near the Church of St. Stephen. The building which is reached by a flight of steps is characterized by an arcade on the ground floor; here there once stood a fortress which dated back to the Angevin period (XIVth century) and which later underwent radical changes and restructuring. Inside the building the *Ethnological Centre of Capri* can be found. Here one finds significant documentation relative to the sculptures and Neolithic ceramics, collections of fossils and interesting archaeological finds discovered in the soil of Capri. A great amount of the material on show here was discovered by the doctor and naturalist Ignazio Cerio who was amongst the first to undertake excavation work at the beginning of this century.

THE MEDIEVAL DISTRICT - All around the famous Small Piazza and beyond the Church of St. Stephen, a complex maze of lanes and narrow alleys testify the presence of a medieval borough at Capri. This enchanting district makes up one of the most exhaustive pictures of the whole island, thanks to the buildings, to the setting out of the town and to the architectural techniques adopted during the Medieval period, offering at the same time a faithful reconstruction of town layout and structure which is common to Southern Italy and in particular to the Campana region.

The small houses which are almost superimposed on one another are separated, by small lanes, along which one can walk with difficulty, where the slopes alternate with the descents and which all join up in large open spaces where other roads meet, these latter lanes being characterized by flights of steps, by graceful arches which succeed one another or by long and dark covered lanes which are rendered all the more suggestive by shops and workshops.

Once again the dominant colour is the whiteness of the house fronts, which are for the greater part built of calcareous stone and tufaceousa material. This uniformity is sometimes broken by the large patches of an intense azure of the almost unreal sky of Capri, whilst the greenness of the vegetation seen in the hedges, in the bowers and in the lush gardens, rich in Mediterranean species and thriving examples of cactai here seems to come into its own.

Amongst the most important architectural buildings of the Medieval district we find the 17th century **Church of Salvatore**, built by Dionisio Lazzari, which, with the adjoining *Convent of the Tertiary*, forms a structural unity which is typical of the XVII th century. The picturesque small **Church of St. Anna** (XIIth century) looks out onto a small courtyard and in fact makes up a structural unity with the adjoining houses.

Alleyways and narrow streets intersect one another in a continuum of ups and downs, underpasses and archways, and tiny white-walled homes alternating with of the characteristic shops in the evocative medieval quarter of Capri.
Facing page, a view the typical architecture of Capri.

FAMOUS HOTELS - A stone's throw from the Piazzetta the Via Vittorio Emanuele stands one of the widest roads of the historical centre of Capri and it in fact divides the Medieval quarter from the area of the famous hotels. The road ends right in front of the Grand Hotel Quisisana where the Via Camerelle and the Via F. Serena begin. Along these two streets, which lead one to the *Belvedere of Tragara* and the *Gardens of Augustus* respectively, can be found other luxury hotels. These streets are characterized by the extremely pretty buildings and by the graceful elegance of the architectural lines which, even though they echo the forms of building common to all Mediterranean islands, are not without their own majesty and grandeur.

In the last ten years Capri's importance as a tourist spot has increased enormously, not only during the tourist season but also during the winter months and notably during the Christmas holidays and New Year when it is possible to take part in the folkloristic displays, enlivened by the unique sound of the putipu. These holidays and visits to the island, along with the Easter holidays and the so-called "weekend" tourism all form to contribute an important economic incentive for the island, and render the streets of the town centre if not overcrowded at least nearly always full of people.

Together with the famous hotels one can also find along these streets, as with many other in the town, characteristic shops selling handicrafts and refined and exclusive boutiques where it is possible to buy the best products on the market, along with the classic characteristic souvenirs of Capri; ceramics, majolica, coral, artisan products made of cord. The epicurean only has the embarrassment of choosing what he would like to eat at the shops and the ice-cream parlours which produce excellent (and usually homemade) ice-cream. Amongst the curiosities which this part of the island holds it should be remembered that in 1905, during excavation work carried out on the foundations of the Grand Hotel Quisisana, important archaeological and paleantological objects were found.

THE GARDENS OF AUGUSTUS - This green park, shaded by the pine trees and brightened up by the presence of many species of flowers, palm trees and other forest trees is a "breathing space" situated not far from the town centre. Its pleasant position which dominates the underlying complex of the *Certosa of St. James*, where the Via Krupp winds steeply up from the Marina Piccola, makes it an ideal resting place for tourists and travellers. From a nearby look out post one can look out onto the marine horizon, a view which embraces one of the most important panoramic sights of the coast of Capri with its incredible variety of steep rocky inlets and which is marked by cliffs near which the imposing and fascinating outline of the *Faraglioni* rises up out of the waters.

VIA KRUPP - The panoramic road, which can only be undertaken on foot because of its narrow dimensions is one of the most noted attractions of this pleasant Mediterranean "gem". It was built at the beginning of this century by the famous German industrialist whose name has been given to the road itself. Picturesquely cut into the rocks which characterize the rocky cliffs of the southern coast of Capri, it goes from the *Gardens of Augustus* to *Marina Piccola*. Those who love Capri will not fail to miss the spectacular transparency of the turquoise waters of the limpid depths where, here and there, one can catch a glimpse of the submerged rocks. The cliffs that fall sheer down to the sea can be seen in the most enchanting of views, and are covered with the Mediterranean scrub, by the agaves, by the Indian figs and by the everpresent cactai. Further down a Saracean **Tower** commemorates the ancient fights for the possession of the island.

The luxuriant Gardens of Augustus.
Facing page, Via Vittorio Emanuele with its boutiques,
shops, and luxury hotels.

THE COLOURS OF THE SUNSET - The magic suggestions of the idyllic island of Capri stand out in a series of imperceptable yet fundamental nuances which are revealed throughout the whole day. One shouldn't forget that light is the fundamental essence of Capri: on this island, this element gives the necessary and indispensibile characteristics needed to enjoy its unspeakable beauty to the full. There is amongst the many forms of "light" that of the early morning, dazzling and vivid, which exalts the chromatic contrasts between the greenness of the vegetation, the intense azure of the sky and the irredescent reflections of the marine transparent waters. But above all there is the fairytale light of the sunset, with its colours and its pink nuances when the fronts of the splendid villas and the silent streets, immersed in the gardens, acquire a soft and suffused tonality, whilst the passing of the day renews the mythical beauty of Capri.

Via di Tragara in the evocative light of sunset.
Facing page, a view from above of the spectacular
Via Krupp, built by the German steel magnate in the early
20th century.
The switchbacks of the stunning road are perfectly
integrated with the sheer cliffs that fall away into the sea.

The Certosa di San Giacomo, of 14th-century origin, with its distinctive extrados arches.

THE CHARTERHOUSE OF ST. JAMES - This building, seen from above the scenic *Belvedere of the Cannon* reveals features of the monumental magnificence, rendered even more peculiar by the Medieval architectural forms of Capri, and has examples of obvious 17th century influence. The rough and undulating profile of the buildings, with their ample display of curved lines and cupolettes gives the complex the characteristics of a decidedly eastern and vaguely Arabian construction even if the real architectural quality of the Charterhouse is anything but eastern in style.

It is an important testimony of the Dark Ages of the Medieval period, surviving the raids and invasions of the pirates and it is almost hidden in the lowland, immerged in the green and lush vegetation which rises up almost like a wall along the slopes and the surrounding reliefs. The characteristics of the landscape of this spot are difficult to forget: from the thick interlacing of the Mediterranean scrub alternated by maritime pines, agaves, Indian figs and cypresses, stand the residential homes of Capri with their balconies, their wide terraces and their beautiful loggias, whilst here and there patches of the intense azure of the swimming pools of the luxury hotels can be seen.

It seems certain that the place where the modern Charterhouse stands today was one of the few places neglected by the Romans, during the period of major changes which the island underwent, and was neglected because of the numerous constructions, imperial villas and residences for the ruling classes which were being built at this time. It is quite probable that the people who built the Charterhouse wanted to take advantage of the steep, impervious and rocky coast which formed a natural defence wall and was therefore easily defended. The founding of the Charterhouse was sponsered, in the second of the XIVth century by Giacomo Arcucci, secretary to Giovanna I, Queen of Naples and the Counts of Altamura and Minervino. The suggestive forms of the archaic buiding do not do justice to their architects and designers, who are unknown. It soon grew in splendour and economic power, but the Charterhouse was then subjected to desecration and devastation caused by the pirate Dragut (second half of the XVIth century) however it was then restored, enlarged and furnished with a better look-out system so as to anticipate the constant risk represented by the Corsairs who swarmed the waters of the Tyrrhenian Sea. Suppressed by Guiseppe Bonaparte in the first years of the XIXth century, mutilated by the crumbling of the 16th century defense tower, it then went into an irreversible decline and was then subsequently used as penal baths, an institution and a place of military confinement.

It was only in more, recent times that the Charterhouse was restored to its ancient splendour, being used as a centre where congresses on tourism are held and where exhibitions of ancient and contemporary art can be seen.

The most ancient parts of the monastic complex can be found around the *Little Cloisters*, graced by elegant arches which stand on small columns, by cross vaults and brightened up by the oleanders which surround the central well-curb, dominated by the Baroque cusp of the so-called *Clocktower*. This part of the charterhouse, where we can find the *Church* and the *Refectory* imitates the trend of the Cistercian monastic architecture whilst the *Great Cloister*, the product of a 16th century addition, denotes structural affinities with that of the Neapolitan charterhouse of San Martino. The external buildings are the *Store-Rooms*, the Cellars and the *Residence of the Prior*.

The Church, which has only one nave maintains an extremely bare and linear

The great Cloister of the complex, built in the late 1500's.

aspect. Worthy of note is the beautiful doorway, which is Gothic (ogival) in style, in whose lunette is a fresco of the XIVth century depicting *"The Virgin and Child with Saint Brunone and Saint James with Queen Giovanna and Count Arcucci.* The apse, illuminated by a three mullioned window surmounted by quadrilobes, holds fragments of frescoes and stucco ornaments dating from the XVIIth century.

In the buildings near the Church the **Museum of the Charterhouse** can be seen, which contains, amongst other things, sculptures which have been severly corroded by the salt water of the Blue Grotto. Such findings would seem to back the hypothesis that the most famous of the grottoes of Capri was, in Roman times a sort of magnificent temple consecrated to the nymphs and was part of the Imperial Villa of Damecuta. Amongst the other works of art worthy of mention are a series of paintings dating from the XVIIth to the XIXth centuries and also the sinister canvases of the German artist Kurt Willhelm Diefenback. The paintings of this artist, who lived on the island and died here in 1913 are characterized by a dark, gloomy pessimism with evident reference to the sepulchral theme and to the concept of death.

More images of the Certosa of San Giacomo. Below, the frescoes in the vault of the apse of the church and, facing page, the canvases by K. W. Diefenbach in the Certosa's museum, named for the artist.

FARAGLIONI - Emerging from the unfathonable depths of an extraordinary and intensely blue sea, these enigmatic colossi of rocks have always constituted the most famous and popular image of Capri throughout the world. Even though, in other places, other rocks of a similar form and dimension are called by the same name, those of Capri are the *Faraglioni* "par excellence".

Situated in front of the south-eastern coast of the island, they were formed by the age-old erosion of the waters which broke off "walls" of rock from the central body of the island and also formed cracks, cavities grottoes and beautiful natural arches, moreover the relentless action of the erosion which took place can be seen all along the coast of Capri, especially in this region.

Subdivided into *Faraglioni of the Earth*, the *Middle Faraglioni* and the *Outer*

Marvellous examples of rock and natural arches of the "magical" waters around the Faraglioni.

The marvellous rocks and natural arches in the magical waters of the Faraglioni.

Enchanting views of the Natural Arch.

Faraglioni they reach a height of respectively 111,81 and 105 mts. Nearby, in front of the so-called Porto di Tragara, stands the "Scoglio del Monacone". A favourite spot with photographers, they are easily reached by boat and make up one of the obligatory stops of the journey around the island. Their waters, limpid and profound, are a paradise for all those interested in nature and underwater diving; on the outer Faraglione lives the rare *Lacerta coerulea faraglionensis*.

THE NATURAL ARCH - This strange natural phenomenon, together with the Faraglioni and the Grotto of Matermania is one of the most famous tourist spots on this part of the island. One gains access to the Arch by a flight of steps which is cut off by a path frequented by tourists. This itinerary describes a sort of circular trip around Mount Tuoro leading out from the centre of Capri to the houses on the outskirts of Matermania, along via Camerelle, via Tragara and via Matermania. This excursion which permits the tourist to admire in all its wildest beauty the marvellous scenario of the Faraglioni, the evocative southern coast of the island with its picturesque coves, the projections, the inlets and the parts of the island which stretch out into the turquoise marine waters can be highly recommended.

The Natural Arch is the visible remainder of an ancient Karst cavity, destroyed by the landslides which broke up parts of the island. It was moulded by the erosive action of the exogenous agents. Its pleasant position, in the midst of a thick pine forest which reveals glimpses of the sea constitutes one of the most attractive motifs of the whole island.

GROTTO OF MATERMANIA - Following the scenic itinerary which broadens out in front of the natural beauty of the Faraglioni, one goes upwards to the Cove of the Fig Tree, at a height where, stretched out along the narrow Punta di Massullo, the unmistakeable profile of the *Casa Rossa* stands out. This villa was once owned by the Tuscan writer Curzio Malaparte.

A little further ahead a fork in the road leads to the Grotto of Matromania. Also known as the *Grotto of Matermania* it is a natural cavity where the ancient orgiastic customs were practised. These rites were part of the worshipping of the *Mater Magna*, and were also frequently carried out on the Sorrento peninsula at the height of the Imperial Age and were similar to those of Cybele. In its present state the grotto shows the elaborative work which was carried out by the Romans, who reinforced the natural vaults with walls and decorated the grotto with mosaics and stucco work of which only scarse and fragmentory traces remain. The latest archaeological findings would suggest that the grotto was used as a temple (where nymphs were worshipped) where the small quantities of water which oozed out of the rocky vaults collected.

The Grotto di Matermània, in which orgiastic rites were celebrated during the Imperial Age.
Facing page, Punta di Massullo with the villa of Curzio Malaparte.

On the following pages, a view of the Scoglio del Monacone with on the right the Faraglioni and the port of Tragara, where the remains of the ancient Roman landing are still visible.

MARINA PICCOLA - This evocative town is one of the most well equipped and fashionably famous seaside resorts of Capri, as well as being a small landing place for the nautical enthusiasts and tourists who have the possibility of mooring their crafts here, along a naturally protected and sheltered coastline. Marina Piccola is symmetrical to Marina Grande since it constitutes the main landing place and the principal port of call for navigational services.

Marina Piccola has its own particular character, more cosy, graceful and attractive, alongside its delightful coves. Between the 1950-1960's the reputation of Capri as a tourist Mecca flourished. This "boom" was thanks to the presence on the island of the most famous names of the film-world, the cultural world and that of show business.

However there are numerous indications that the place was populated as far back as the most remote ages. Along the rocky spurs which are outlined along the eastern side of Mount Solaro, one finds the *Grotto of the Ferns* which dominates the underlying Marina and which represents one of the most important prehistoric sites of the whole island. Archeological excavations have brought to light a numerous quantity of domestic objects as well as the remains of funeral objects and primitive ceramic objects. This grotto, populated as far back as the Neolithic Bronze Age, acted as an important lookout post along the southern coast. In the Imperial Age, the Romans used it to reinforce the

The charming Marina Piccola, much frequented in the 1950's and 60's by personalities from the worlds of culture, cinema, and the stage.

Rocks on the southern coast of the island.

characteristics of the natural landing place; some building work done on the ancient Roman port are still visible today near the so-called *Rock of the Sirens*. Today the enchanting vision of Marina Piccola can be enjoyed by those who reach it by means of either the road which bears the same name, or by the evocative Via Krupp. The delightful "Rock of the Sirens" (or "of the Mule") forms a natural barrier between the *Marina di Mulo* which stretches out in a westerly direction up to the Point bearing the same name, and the *Marina di Pennauto* which stretches to the east up to the powerful outline of the Faraglioni. In addition to the numerous tourist and seaside infrastructures Marina Piccola has typical restaurants and fashionable "haunts" such as the famous "Canzone del Mare" ("Song of the Sea") which during the "roaring" years of the Cinema became one of the meeting points for artists of world renown.

Marina Piccola is one of the main starting points from where one sets out (either with one's own personal craft or with the one of the numerous public transport boats) along the journey around the island. This trip allows one to enjoy the considerable scenic beauties of the island, the fascinating outline of its rocky coasts, marked in several places by marvellous natural cavities and by steep and impending cliffs. The boat trip allows one to pass near the Faraglioni, - immense and solitary rocky giants-or even to penetrate in their natural arches through which one can pass.

On this page, two views of Marina Piccola. Top, the bathing establishments and the Scoglio delle Sirene; bottom, bathers on the beach.
Facing page, top, the Torre Saracena at Marina di Pennauto; bottom, the Grotta Rossa.
On the following pages, the Grotta Bianca.

A view of the Castle of Castiglione.

THE CASTLE OF CASTIGLIONE - The climb up to the panoramic spot of Castiglione is without doubt amongst the most worthwhile if only for the enjoyment of the spectacular scenic views which can be seen in the direction of the Faraglione and towards the towns of Capri, which emerge from the Mediterranean scrub, wonderfully set round in the shape of an amphitheatre along the slopes of the natural saddle which separates Marina Grande from Marina Piccola.

This pleasant excursion allows one to observe in all their entirety, the unadulterated buildings of marked Medieval influence which make up one of the most characteristic and important examples of the ancient urban arrangements of the historical centre of Capri. The Castle of Castiglione, as one sees it today has the characteristics bestowed on it by restruction work and by restoration work which was only finished in quite recent times. The powerful embattled ramparts and the huge square reinforcement towers, which are also surmounted by a crown of merlons, stand on the summit of a rocky peak. The side of the building which faces the sea seems to fall in steep crags and cliffs of bare rock in which the gigantic Grotto of Castiglione can be seen, down towards the sea, whilst on the side facing the Charterhouse of St. James is covered by a thick verdant undergrowth, from which some magnificent and typical residences seem to peep out at one.

The Castle of Castiglione was originally a Medieval structure, built on the site of an ancient Greek acropolis. During the numerous pirate raids the Castle was an important defensive rampart for the population of Capri (even though most of the population used to take shelter in the *Grotto of Castiglione*. This grotto, which was once a prehistoric seat since the Neolithic era, was used by the Romans as a temple, connected to an *Imperial Villa* above the grotto. At the Villa one can make out the remains of walls of *opus reticulatum*.

This magnificent villa, which stands on the northern slopes of Castiglione, was discovered at the end of the XVIIIth century by the Austrian archaeologist Norbert Hadrawa. It seems that in numerous rooms, later hidden by a disasterous attempt to cover up the villa, a large amount of interesting and valuable exhibits were found, such as mosaic and marble floors, frescoes and stucco decorations which were unfortunately lost after the plundering of the Villa by Hadrawa himself.

Two panoramic views of the town of Capri.

VILLA JOVIS - The majestic remains of a magnificent Roman villa dating back to the Imperial Age stand above the plateau which culminates in the so-called Mount Tiberius (335 m) The Villa which bears the name of the most important of the Olympian divinities is the most representative of a consistent number of villas built on Capri during the Augustan-Tiberian eras.

A written tradition, quoted by Tacitus would attribute Augustus' successor with the building of twelve imperial residences all dedicated to the Consenting Gods (Jupiter, Apollo, Neptune, Mars, Vulcan, Mercury, Juno, Minerva, Venus, Vesta, Ceres and Diana).

The itinerary which takes one to the important archaeological site is amongst the most trodden and frequented by tourists, not only for the exceptional attraction which this extraordinary testimony of the Roman presence on Capri holds, but also for the halo of mystery, and at the same time, the great and dissolute power which surrounds the figure of Tiberius and the myth surrounding the man which is echoed in the anecdotes heard on the island even today.

From the centre of Capri, first taking the via Sopramonte and then taking the via Tiberius which leads into the via Moneta one can easily reach the spot where the Villa stands. This route runs along a gentle but continuous slope which is characterized by narrow streets flanked by beautiful gardens, parks and residences and rural orchards; here and there one gets marvellous glimpses of the scenery towards Capri and its roofs, brightened by the typical architecture and immersed in the dazzling brightness of the white houses. In the most favourable season the oleanders are in bloom, the leaves of the Indian figs and the characteristic outline of the agaves enliven the walks of the tourists and the visitors who can breathe in the unmistakable perfume of Capri,

The massive ruins that still suggest the original magnificence of the ancient Villa Jovis.

perhaps stopping a minute to contemplate the astonishing qualities of a place which has been so generous to Man.

A little before the ruins of the Villa Jovis, on the right, stand the broken remains of another Roman tower. Here, there once stood a *Lighthouse Tower*, an ancient light system used for signaling by either fire or smoke. During Tiberius' stay on Capri, this structure was particularly important as it permitted the Emperor to have daily communication with the mainland, by means of a beam situated on the facing Punta Campanella, at the extremity of the Sorrento peninsular. In such a way Tiberius decided the destiny of the Empire during the last years of his tormented reign.

From the same tower contact was also kept with the lighthouse of Capo Miseno, in whose roadstead the imperial fleet rode at anchor. Due to a strange coincidence the Lighthouse Tower crumbled during sismic tremors a little while before the death of Tiberius; it was later restored and used as a lighthouse to defend the ships of the island up until the XVIIth century.

There have been many discussions about the figure of Tiberius, discussions which more often than not linger over details of his supposed vices and perversions rather than on his virtues and qualities as a ruler of the boundless Empire of Rome. We should not forget however, that many of the anecdotes, which refer to the successor of Augustus, whether they are true or not, are, the result of stories told by narrators who were clearly biased and definitely hostile towards Tiberius. It would therefore be appropriate to reflect, separating fiction from fact, on the terrible punishments which he inflicted on families and servants whom he felt were unloyal, on the capital punishments carried out by throwing his enemies into a bottomless abyss (known today as *Tiberius'*

On the following pages, a reconstruction of the Imperial Villa.

1. ENTRANCE
2. VESTIBULE
3. BATHS
4. HALL
5. RESERVOIR
6. IMPERIAL QUARTERS
7. CHURCH OF S.M. DEL SOCCORSO
8. IMPERIAL LOGGIA
9. TRICLINIUM
10. KITCHEN
11. TERRACE
12. SPECULARIUM

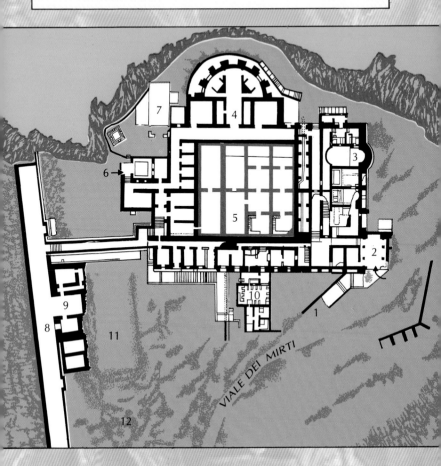

Leap) as well as the slaughtering of young men and women which took place in the Blue Grotto after the licentious erotic games in which both sexes took part. Concerning these facts Axel Munthe writes ("*The History of Villa St. Michael*" Publishers: Garzanti, 1940) "As to the sinister traditions of Tiberius, handed down through the ages by the *Annals* of Tacito the "detractor of humanity" as Napoleon called him, I said to Lord Dufferin that History had never made such a big mistake as when it condemned this great Emperor to such infamy only on the testimony of his greatest accusors. Tacito is a splendid writer but his *Annals* are historical fiction, not History... That Tacito himself didn't believe the stories about the orgies on Capri is clear from his own narritive, since he doesn't play down to even one degree his general conception of Tiberius as a great Emperor and as a great man "of admirable character and much respected" to use his own words. Even his much less intelligent follower, Svetonio recounts the most filthy stories, making the observations that it is hardly admissable that they should be told let alone believed... Tiberius was 68 when he retired to Capri with a reputation for having led a strict and moral life still intact, and not even damaged by his worst enemies. The possible diagnosis of senile dementia can be excluded, because all the historians maintain that the old man was in full possession of his faculties and was physically fit up until his death at the age of 79. Moreover the streak of madness which ran through Giuliano's family was absent in that of Claudio. His life on the island was that of a solitary old man, of a tired ruler of an ungrateful world, a gloomy

More images of Villa Jovis,
built by the emperor Tiberius.
Below, a detail of the grandiose cisterns.
Facing page, a detail of the kitchen area.

idealist with a shattered and bitter heart (today one could call him a hypercondiriac), but a man with a magnificent intellect and rare spirit still having faith in humanity. It is little wonder that he had no trust in his contemporaries and that he hated them because almost all the men and women in whom he had put his trust had betrayed him...".

The principle nucleus of Villa Jovis or *Palazzo di Tiberio* stands on the summit of the most extreme eastern slope of Capri, in a scenario of inexpressible beauty. Above the ruins rises the small *Church of St. Maria del Soccorso* built on the site of a medieval place of worship dedicated to *St. Christopher* and *St. Leonard*. Nearby is a statue of *The Virgin and Child*, from where one can look out over the whole island, taking in the endless horizon which sweeps from the distant Ischia to the Neapolitan gulf dominated by the characteristic profile of Vesuvius, as far as the nearby Punta Campanella and the wide gulf of Salerno.

The main part of the ancient imperial construction revolves around the mangnifent complex of the *water tanks* which were used to provide water for the entire complex of the Villa collecting the rain water in spacious impluvia. All around are to be found the various interiors which have been discovered and which have a total surface area of over 7000 square metres; it is believed however that the Villa Jovis with its various outlying buildings covered an even vaster area. Particularly interesting are the remains of the wall which sometimes show elements of *opus reticulatum* and sometimes elements of

On these pages, more images
of the ruins of Tiberius' villa, the
most important archaeological
complex on the island of Capri.
The architecture of the villa,
which extends below the small
church of Santa Maria del
Soccorso for more than 7,000
square meters, adapts to the
steep slope thanks to its
esplanades and panoramic
terraces.

The ruins of the semicircular hall of Villa Jovis.

opus incertum, whilst often the floors have a herring-bone pattern (*opus spicatum*). At the side of the water tanks the actual *imperial residence* is situated, which leads to the so-called *imperial loggia*. The latter which has a triclinium and exedrae was the spot favoured by Tiberius for his walks.

Another conspicuous portion of the villa is the *baths* which show the classical division of the Roman thermal constructions: *Apodyterium* (changing room), *Frigidarium*, *Tepidarium*, and *Calidarium*. A complex heating system (hypocaust) was used to heat the waters. Next to the church of St. Maria di Soccorso, right at the edge of the rocky slopes which fall sheer to the sea are the remains of what has mistakenly been called a *Temple* (where nymphs were worshipped). In reality this was a hemicircular room used as a meeting place where the imperial chancellery held audience.

In a position set apart from the complex of imperial buildings, one can see the ruins of what must have been the kitchens and store houses of the Villa. A little further away from the main part of the Villa, near the steep slope which descends to Marina Grande can be seen the ruins of massive walls and vaulted constructions. In all probability these are the ruins of a *Specularium* (Observatory) which was also used to communicate with the lighthouses on the coast of the Campana region.

THE BATHS OF TIBERIUS - The conspicuous remains emerging from the turquoise transparency of the marine waters which run along the front of the northern coast of the island, in harmony with the so-called *Houses of the Palace on the Sea* constitute a visible testimony of the marine quarters of a magnificent imperial Villa of the Augustean age. The traces of the Baths of Tiberius which can be visited today consist of a sloping wall which leans against a slope rich in vegetation but liable to slide down; of a small area destined to be used a dwelling place; of a temple with adjoining exedra, used for fish production and some service structures for a small landing stage suitably defended by walls against the disintegrating action of the breakers.

Many modifications and transformations carried out over the centuries and the complete absence of a large central nucleus do not allow one to immediately perceive the exact location of the original *Palatium* (palace) of Augustus. We know for certain that the emperor had a soft spot for the place which is today occupied by the Houses of the Palace on the Sea and that the villa which stood here was certainly more sober and less imposing than the sumptuous propor-

The Bath of Tiberius, and the ruins of the small Roman port.

*The Baths of Tiberius. The beach and bathers and a
panoramic view from the Loggiato of Villa San Michele.*

tions of the villa that his successor, Tiberius, raised on the brink of the steep
precipices which face the Sorrento peninsular.

The *Villa of the Palace on the Sea* is the only one of the numerous imperial
villas which is situated close to the sea and which occupies a marittime position
as opposed to the traditional elevated positions favoured by the Roman architects who worked on Capri.

Fragmentary archaeological findings which have come to light have shown us
the characteristics of a country residence, with wide spaces set apart for
gardens and for the emperor's walks. Today the Tiberian foundations which
are known as the Baths of Tiberius are the only parts which have withstood
the onslaught of time and the thoughtless plundering by the Austrian Hadrawa
in the 18th century, stripping the Villa of the Palace on the Sea of many ar-
chitetonic furnishings and artistic decorations. Afterwards, during the 19th
century the area was used as a military base by the French and the English
who further contributed to the ruining of this important archaeological site
which today is populated by private residences, hotels and rural dwellings.

Boats nearing the entrance to the Grotta Azzurra, the karst cavity known throughout the world for the magical atmosphere created by the extraordinary plays of light within it.
The Grotta, like the Faraglioni, is a compulsory stop for anyone who visits the island.

THE BLUE GROTTO - The Blue Grotto is counted as being one of the major tourist attractions of Capri. This Karst cavity, together with the equally famous Faraglioni has contributed in spreading the enigma of this island all over the world. The most traditional and evocative way of carrying out this excursion, which shouldn't be missed during the course of a visit to Capri, is to take one of the tourist boats or motorboats from the Marina Grande. The visit to the Blue Grotto, which can only be undertaken if weather and sea conditions permit should take place, if at all possible, in the morning so that one can enjoy the play of light which reflects the marvellous chromatic effects of underscribable fascination and evocativeness. It would be very wise to avoid the guided tours with the inevitable overcrowding mass of tourists during certain periods of the year (National Holidays, long week-ends and the high season) as there will bound to be long queues at the embarkation points and outside the entrance to the Blue Grotto, as well as a marked decline in the evocative effect obtained inside the grotto, due to the presence of too many overcrowded boats of noisy tourists.

The Blue Grotto which was a well-known and favourite place with the Romans, fell into oblivion and it became shrouded in fear, mystery and superstition blown out of all proportion by the inhabitants of the island who were convinced that the grotto was a meeting place for witches and that horrifying monsters lived there. It seems quite probable however that an increase of the

bradysismic phenomenon almost closed off the access to the grotto.

It was already the subject of much discussion with both scholars and map-readers as far back as the XVIIth century and was then rediscovered in 1826 by two daring and bold German travellers, the writer A. Kopisch and the painter E. Fries. Since those days a constant and endless stream of visitors and tourists have visited the place as well as a great number of Italian and foreign literary scholars, who have drawn inspiration from the place.

Outside the grotto, whilst waiting patiently to pass through the narrow entrance way, it is possible to observe the remains of the *Villa of Gràdola*. This building, also known as the *Villa of Gradelle* is a Roman construction of secondary importance if one compares it with other, more conspicuous traces of the Imperial era. For a while it lent its name to the grotto which lies below it, before this became known by the name which extols its predominant colours. However the particular predominance that the more well-known imperial residence of the *Villa of Damecuta* assumed in this would support the hypothesis that the Blue Grotto was used by the Romans as a marine temple (where nymphs were worshipped). Such a hypothesis is strengthened by the presence of building work of the Roman period found inside the grotto and by the discovery of sculptures submerged by the bradysismic actions and corroded by the sea water. Today these statues can be seen inside the Charterhouse Museum of St. James.

The atmosphere of magic seduction inside the Blue Grotto is obtained by the sky-blue reflections of the beams of light which penetrate through the narrow access hole, whilst the extraordinary cobalt-blue transparencies are caused by the light diffused under the mirror of the waters and which filters through an underwater opening. This opening was probably a primeval cavity submerged during ancient tectonic upheavals.

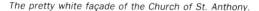

The pretty white façade of the Church of St. Anthony.

THE PHOENICIAN FLIGHT OF STEPS - In spite of its name which refers explicitly to the Phoenicians — who definitely lived on the island and used it as a commercial landing place along their routes in the lower Tyrrhenian Sea — this impervious rocky flight of steps is one of the few proven surviving traces of the Greek colonization of the island.

The walk which consists of over 800 steps cut into the bare rock climbs up the north-eastern buttresses of Mount Solaro and has for centuries been the only means of communication between Anacapri, the rest of the island and more importantly with the landing wharfs of Marina Grande.

The achievement, during the last century, of a means of communciation between the two main centres of Capri and Anacapri has granted the Phoenician Flight of Steps the role of a tourist route, still trodden by fishermen and tourists who would like to discover the landscape marvels of the island along this ancient rocky itinerary which, however tiring, allows one to enjoy a more direct and natural relationship with the unparalleled environment of Capri.

The Scala Fenicia (Phoenician Flight of Steps).

ANACAPRI

Splendidly set out along the gentle slopes which descend from the steep sides of Mount Solaro, the second most important centre on Capri is set out like on oil stain on the vast thickly-cultivated plateau, in a context of shimmering Mediteranean beauty. It was an elevated settlement during the Greek presence on the island and was a favourite haunt of the patricial Roman families who built numerous villas here; loved and frequented by Tiberius who spent many long periods at the imperial villa of Damecuta, it was also chosen by the illustrious Swedish humanist and doctor Axel Munthe as a home. Munthe, in his *The History of St. Michael*" has wonderfully captivated and handed down to the following generations, the image of this oneeric and fairytale-like enchanted island.

Even today, in spite of transformations undergone due to the huge numbers of tourists, Anacapri has managed to retain its characteristics as a typically elevated centre on a Mediterranean island. The white houses, with their decidedly "Caprese" architectural lines, are set out in their bright splendour (given to them by the whitewashed fronts, by the airy and luminous terraces, by the often curvilinear volutes of the roofs of the buildings). All around, a lush vegetation betrayed by the gardens, by the orchards and by the bowers can be

A panoramic view of Anacapri. On the facing page, the Loggiato of Villa San Michele with the ancient sphinx.

seen, whilst the neighbouring districts are marked by the presence of myrtle, juniper, lentisk, broom and by various other species, alternating with the maritime pine and the Aleppo pine.

Anacapri is an ideal holiday village and a renowned health resort which enjoys the benefits of an extraordinary mild and healthy climate. As a starting point for interesting naturalistic excursions and also history trips, it is clustered around the beautiful **Parish Church of St. Sophia**. This was built during Medieval times and is brightened up by the central cupola, by the small minor cupolas and by the majestic *Clocktower*. The elegant Baroque facade (XVIIIth century) in two orders is vertically divided by pilaster strips.

VILLA ST. MICHAEL - The architectonically eclectic and extremely heterogeneous construction is situated in the town of Capodimonte, on the edge of a steep slope which falls sheer to the underlying Baths of Tiberius. Included within a fantastic landscape context which offers aspects of touching pleasantness, it stands out thanks to the brightness of its composite architectonic attitude amongst the arrogant greenness of the lush Mediterranean vegetation and the cobalt-blue patches of the marine waters below.

On the site where Axel Munthe started to build the villa, from 1896 stood a rural dwelling which even today, even if it has been transformed, makes up the central nucleus of the buildings. During excavation work, a great number of the remains of the buildings dating back to the Imperial times were discovered; even today the conspicuous remains of the walls of *opus reticulatum* would support the theory that this site was the ancient seat of the *Villa of Capodimonte*, one of the 12 imperial residences of Augustean-Tiberiean foundation.

The entrance of Villa St. Michael.

THE CASTLE OF BARBAROSSA

THE CASTLE OF BARBAROSSA - The imposing turreted ruins of the Castle of Barbarossa appear in all their glory and turn one's gaze to beyond the scenic terraces of the Villa St. Michael. Due to its spectacular and impregnable position on the summit of a steep rocky crag this castle has been throughout the centuries an eagle's nest from where one could look out onto the endless green horizons and towards the coast of the region of Campana.

Some architectonic details such as the small chapel with apses which can still be made out within the main bulk of the buildings, support the hypothesis that this ancient castle, at least originally, formed part of a fortified structure built by the Byzantium race. The castle's name recalls the pirate raids carried out by Barbarossa who in 1535 overcame its defences, carrying out the worst pillages that the island ever suffered.

Behind the nickname of Barbarossa is hidden the real identity of Khair-ad-Din admiral and Turkish pirate born in Mitilene, who lived between the 15th and the 16th centuries. The famous Corsair who together with his brothers attacked the Aegian and north African coasts, finally establishing a small kingdom in Algiers which was the starting point for the pirate raids through the whole Mediterranean basin. After having conquered Tunisia (1533) he was given command of the Ottoman fleet by the Turkish sovreign Solimano. Solimano often blocked the fleet of Charles Vth as well as those of Genoa and Venice obtaining a position of superiority over the Christian fleet on the waters, culminating in the Battle of Lepanto (1571).

A view of the Castle of Barbarossa.

The white facade of the 18th-century church of San Michele and a detail of its interior, with the valuable "Garden of Eden" maiolica floor decoration (shown in detail on the following pages).

THE CHURCH OF ST. MICHAEL - This building stands out due to its Baroque facade in two orders which holds elements of considerable architectonic interest and has an undulating trend, rendered by the little arch above the main archway and by the coloumns of the ground floor. The upper portion of the facade is scanned by pilaster strips in the vertical sense, culminating in further small decorations in the form of long pyramids, whilst at the centre of the "crown" of the building stands a triangular structure. The interior, with its central hexagonal plan is considered to be one of the most marvellous architectonic and decorative masterpieces of the whole Campania region. This place of worship, was completed in 1719, based on a plan of the architect, painter and sculptor, Antonio Vaccaro, born in Naples and who lived between the XVII and the XVIIIth centuries.

The masterpiece of this church is the incredible majolica floor which the Abruzzese artist Leonardo Chiaiese carried out, probably under the auspices of Vaccaro and which depicts magnificently some allegorical biblical tales such as the *Earthly Paradise* and the *Expulsion form the Garden of Adam and Eve.*

Three images of Monte Solaro at flowering time for the broom that colors its slopes.
The view from the overlook of this mountain is enchanting.
On the facing page, a statue of the emperor Augustus at the Fortino di Bruto, with the Faraglioni in the background.

CABLECAR AND MOUNT SOLARO - The highest mountain summit along the relief of Capri (589 mts) can be reached on foot and starts off from Anacapri, crossing the cultivated slopes of the mountain and crossing the lush Mediterranean vegetation. For the laziest of travellers, a cablecar takes one directly from Anacapri to the summit from which one can make out some ruins of ancient fortified structures, built by the English.

From the scenic look-out post one can look out over the enchanting views of the Neapolitan gulf towards Ischia, dominated by the characteristic outline of Epomeo, towards the bridging islands, towards Naples laid out at the feet of Vesuvius and beyond the Sorrento peninsular as far as the Apennine mountains. Below lies Capri, whitened by the slopes of the saddle which precipitates into the sea with its rocky crags, whilst from the cobalt blue of its waters rises the gigantic and enigmatic outline of the group of rocks known as the Faraglioni.

The not too distant hermitage of *St. Maria a Cetrella* merits a visit. The delightful 14th century architecture recalls the forms of the typical Caprese architecture and stands on the edge of the steep precipice which faces the Marina Piccola. The story which says that the the building is based on the site of an ancient Greek temple consecrated to the worshipping of Venus and Citerea seems to have no actual proof.

THE WATCHTOWER - The characteristic cylindrical outline of this stone tower stands at the limit of the rocky crags which face the Punta Carena. This fortified structure would also seem to have an important strategic role throughout the last century when it constituted one of the main defense structures of the apparatus used to guard the plains of Anacapri. Even today the tourist has the opportunity to visit the ruins which represent the indelible historic reminder of this part of the island. The remains of ancient fortresses, of castles, of towers and of look-out posts can be seen along the vast plateau which as a border, has only the eastern slopes of Mount Solaro.

The excursion on foot can be highly recommended as far as the *Belvedere of the Migliara*; from this exceptional panoramic point it is possible to admire the wild profile of the coast of Capri, which in this part of the island is rendered particularly evocative by the scenic presence of the rocks of *Marmolata*, which rise up in the manner of fantastic Dolomite rocks.

The Watchtower dominates the steep and rugged precipice.

The Tower of Materita stands out from the thick Mediterranean vegetation.

THE TOWER OF MATERITA - What is commonly called the tower of Materita is, in fact, one of the most beautiful residences on Capri. The building, entirely crowned with merlons and surmounted by a beautiful tower is softened on both sides by elegant bifores. Above, the circle of merlons is sustained by an interlacing of overhanging brackets. The tranquil solitude of this place, surrounded by an olive grove and vines in the midst of a small cypress wood and lush vegetation inspired Axel Munthe, who here, finished his book "*The History of St. Michael*".

In his masterpiece, speaking of Materita, he wrote (op. cit. Publishers: Garzanti, 1940) "I have finally accepted my destiny. I am too old to fight with a God. I have retired and have come to my fortress, to the old towers where I intend to resist for the last time. Dante was still alive when the friars began work on the Torre di Materita which is half monastery, half fortress as solid as the rock on which it stands. "There is no greater sorrow than to remember happy times in times of sadness". How many times has this bitter phrase echoed around the walls since I've come here! But after all, was the Florentine right? Is it true that there is no greater sorrow that to remember past happiness in times of sorrow? I don't think so. It is with joy and not with sorrow that my thoughts go back to St. Michael, where the happiest years of my life were spent. But it is true that I no longer like to go there: I feel as if I am intruding on sacred ground, a sacred past that will never return, when the world was young and the sun was my friend.

It is bliss to wander along in the soft light, under the olives of Materita. It is lovely to sit and meditate about the old tower and it is the one and only thing which I can do... The tower looks eastwards, to where the sun sets.

Soon the sun will sink into the sea, then twilight will come and then the night. It has been a lovely day...".

The tower which was originally built in the XVth century and constituted an integral part of the coastal defense structure against the threat of the pirate raids was bought and restored by the Swedish writer who loved it and used it as a place for reflection and meditation. Even today the interiors hold a large number of interesting works of art, memorabilia and souvenirs connected with the stay of Axel Munthe on Capri.

VILLA DI DAMECUTA - The flat plains of Damecuta stretch out along the north-western portion of the vast plateau of Anacapri. In the Imperial Roman era this area was chosen by the architects of the capital who built a great number of villas and residences here. In virtue of its excellent geographical position, and its pleasant exposition to the rays of the sun and to the sea breezes the area around Damecuta soon became a residential area for the patriarchial Roman families. Amongst the many buildings, several of which were in fact farms, those of *Aiano, Montivello, Tiberino* and *Vitareto* stand out.

Ruins in "opus reticulatum" of the Villa of Damecuta.

A view of the Tower of Damecuta.

Along the margin of this idyllic scenario on the plateau of Anacapri near the Medieval Tower of Damecuta lies the vast archaeological area which has rendered traces of one of the most imposing and magnificent Roman villas of the Imperial period: the Villa Damecuta. The origins of the place name seem to be lost in the times of the Greek colonization of the island; the hypothesis that Damecuta seems to be derived from *Domus Augusti* seems to have no foundation in fact.

The complex visissitudes of this great imperial building, haunted by the figure of Tiberius and his myth, obscure and worrying but at the same time luminous and fascinating were brought to light at the beginning of the second half of the 1930's. At that time the generosity of Axel Munthe, the owner of the place, allowed the archeologists to procede with the work of salvaging the remains of the ancient building.

It also seems certain that this villa was the first of the Imperial villas of the island to be abandoned; seriously lesioned by the fall of materials of a piroclastic nature from the eruptions of Vesuvius, during the destructive episodes which wiped out Pompeii, Ecolano and Stabia (79 B.C.) almost completely submerged by the volcanic material, it fell into decline. Afterwards it underwent frequent pillaging and plundering throughout the ages and also underwent destruction during its transformation into a military base for the Bourbons and for the English who stripped it of its considerable architectural patrimony. This building, as others on the island must have had a large number of ornaments, pictures, stucco work sculptures, mosaic or marble floors.

Today it offers a place for contemplation for visitors especially the work in *opus reticulatum*, whilst in other places can be found the more simple examples of *opus incertum*. In particular the *Loggia* stands out, facing the steep panoramic brink which falls sheer down to the underlying marine abysses. This was the favourite place of the Emperor for his walks, and is enriched by numerous exedrae. A little below the embattled Tower of Damecuta a strong fortress in stone blocks, built during the XIIth century so as to guard over the moves of the Corsair boats lies the imperial *Domus*. Here in what must have been the bedroom of the Emperor an acephaleos bust has been found depicting *Narcissus* (nude) a clear example of the refined tastes of Tiberius and his lascivious leanings. It seems certain that the Villa had a flight of steps which led down to the sea, near the modern day Punta di Gradola and near the entrance to the Blue Grotto, where the remains of another Roman villa are clearly visible.

A TASTE OF CAPRI

Neapolitan gastronomy privileges fundamentally simple ingredients which, alone, with their unmistakable flavor, and perhaps with the help of spices or the herbs long found in abundance in the Neapolitan countryside, can give a dish a uniquely distinct personality. The recipes created are based on freshness, genuineness, intensity of flavour, and are always faithful to the dictum of avoiding excessive mixture of dissimilar ingredients. Think, for example, of the sunny freshness of the tomato, the tasty *fiordilatte* (cow's milk mozzarella), or the ability to draw out subtlest and most valuable fragrances from the fish caught in the Tyrrhenian Sea, and the meats of animals nourished by crops from the countryside of Campania. Helped by such a satisfying environment, Neapolitan cuisine has been able to take its pick when creating the recipes destined to become traditional over the centuries: fish, meat, vegetables, and the more famous specialities like pasta, with a particular predilection for spaghetti, and pizza, which has now become, throughout the world, a stereotyped symbol not only of Naples but of Italy as a whole.

And if pizza is the Neapolitan dish par excellence, it lacks no rivals when it comes to variety. Alongside of the traditional "Margherita" and "Neapolitan" pizzas, or the typical "white pizza with escarole" there are literally countless other varieties. Italian, international and even exotic recipes have transformed this disk of dough – the brainchild of Neapolitan cooks – into an "ideal space" where anyone can use his imagination to the full and satisfy all his most extravagant cravings.

All the recipes are for four servings.

Clam Sauté

3 lb clams
2 tomatoes
$^1/_2$ cup olive oil

2 cloves garlic
Parsley
White wine, I glass

Soak the clams in salted water for at least 4 hours to remove all the sand. Drain well. Sauté the garlic in a skillet and add the clams, sprinkle with a little chopped parsley, cover and cook for a few minutes. Check the clams and remove them as they open, and set them aside.

When all the clams are open, put them back into the skillet. Add the fresh tomatoes cut into chunks, and the white wine, cook over a moderate flame. As soon as the clams are hot, remove from the stove, garnish with chopped parsley and serve.

Ravioli Capri Style

For the pasta:
4 cups flour
2 tablespoons extra-virgin olive oil
2 cups water

For the filling:
2 eggs
3/4 lb dry *caciotta* cheese
1/2 lb Parmesan cheese
Marjoram

For the sauce :
Fresh tomato sauce with basil

Mince the Parmesan and *caciotta* cheeses finely; add the eggs and 2–3 tablespoons marjoram, and mix thoroughly. Allow the mixture to stand while you prepare the pasta. Make a well with the flour; work in the hot water and the oil until the dough is can be rolled in a ball and comes clean in the hands. Let it stand, covered, for about one hour, then knead again for a few minutes. Roll out the dough on a floured surface until it is paper-thin. On one half of the sheet of dough, place teaspoonfuls of the filling mixture at uniformly spaced intervals, then cover with the other half of the sheet. Use a ravioli cutter to cut out the ravioli. Cook in boiling salted water. Traditionally, these ravioli are served with fresh tomato sauce with basil.

Tortiglioni with Clams

12 oz whole wheat tortiglioni
2 $^1/_2$ lb clams
1 clove garlic, crushed

2 green onions
Dry white wine
Olive oil

If you buy the clams the night before you use them, or early in the morning, to keep them fresh wrap them in a wet dish towel and put them in the coolest part of your refrigerator, but not the freezer.

The best way to eliminate the sand in the clams is to soak them in lightly salted water. Place a dish, upside down in the bottom of the bowl with the salted water. As if by magic, the sand from the clams will collect under the dish. Change water 2 or 3 times until there is no trace of sand. Since most clams come from "farms," the sand is finer than normal sea sand and you may need to change the water more than 3 times, but it is well worth the effort. Discard the dead clams, the ones that don't open partly in the clean water, and obviously those that don't open when heated. Scoundrels!!

Clean and slice the onions. Put the rinsed clams into a pan with a little olive oil and the garlic. Heat over a high flame until they open, douse with half a glass of white wine and cook until the wine evaporates.

Turn off the flame, remove the clams (set them aside and keep them hot), and the garlic. You may have to strain the liquid through cheesecloth if the clams were not perfectly rinsed.

Cook the tortiglioni in boiling salted water until they are *al dente*. Put them in the pan with the liquid from the clams and cook over a high flame for a few minutes. Turn off the flame, add the sliced onions and mix. Add the clams in their open shells and serve. This is a fragrant and original dish, but remember, no cheese, please!

87

Sea Bass "all'acqua pazza"

2 lb fish (bass or gilthead), cleaned
5–6 plum or cherry tomatoes

$^1/_2$ cup olive oil
1–2 cloves garlic, chopped
1 sprig parsley, chopped
$^1/_2$ hot red pepper, chopped

Place the fish in a large skillet. Cut the tomatoes in half and put them in the skillet along with the garlic, parsley and hot red pepper. Cover with aluminum foil so that no steam can escape and cook over a low flame.

When the fish is tender, salt to taste.

Place the fish on a serving platter and flavor with the cooking liquid.

Caponata

4 rounds dry whole bread, "freselle"
1 lb ripe tomatoes
$^1/_2$ cup olive oil

2 large cloves garlic
5–6 basil leaves
Oregano

Quickly moisten the "freselle" with water, then rub with garlic and salt to taste.

Place them in a large salad bowl, add the sliced tomatoes, oregano and chopped garlic.
Sprinkle generously with olive oil and mix well; wait about 30 minutes before serving.
This classic caponata can be enriched and varied according to your taste. There are several ingredients you can add such as anchovies, tuna fish, green or black olives, fresh celery, onion, and sliced hard-boiled egg, making it a tasty main dish.

Capri Salad

1–3 tomatoes	Olive oil
14 oz fresh	6–7 basil leaves
mozzarella cheese	Oregano

Cut the mozzarella into medium-thick slices.
Slice the tomatoes to about the same thickness.
Alternate the cheese and tomato slices on individual plates, garnish with basil leaves and season with a dash of salt and oregano, and extra-virgin olive oil.

Babà

13 oz flour
2 oz sugar
3 eggs

8 oz butter
1 oz brewer's yeast
1 glass milk

For the syrup:
4 oz sugar
The peel of one lemon
1 glass rum
2-$\frac{1}{2}$ cups water

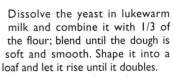

Dissolve the yeast in lukewarm milk and combine it with 1/3 of the flour; blend until the dough is soft and smooth. Shape it into a loaf and let it rise until it doubles.

In the meantime beat the eggs, grease a tube pan with butter, and soften the rest of the butter.

Pour the flour on work table and combine all the ingredients with the risen loaf.

Knead thoroughly and delicately. Put the dough in the greased pan, filling it to 1/3 of its capacity. Cover and let rise. When the dough reaches 2/3 of the pan's capacity, bake in a moderate oven until it rises and is done inside (a knife or toothpick inserted in the middle should come out clean); raise the oven temperature to 375°F and continue baking until golden.

Remove the cake from the oven and let it cool in the pan; turn it out when it has cooled completely.

While it is baking, prepare the syrup. Boil the water with the sugar and the lemon peel, until it thickens.

Remove from the stove and set aside; when it has cooled a little, add the rum and stir well. Pour it over the cooled baba gradually until it is fully absorbed.

Torta Caprese

1 lb shelled almonds
1 cup sugar
9 oz semi-sweet chocolate
1 cup + 1 tablespoon butter
10 eggs

2 oz plain cookies or rusks
Rum
2 tablespoons confectioners' sugar
1 teaspoon powdered cinnamon

Separate the eggs. Beat the whites until stiff and set aside; beat the yolks with the sugar until light. Chop the almonds, chocolate, and cookies or rusks in a food processor until fine; add one spoonful at a time to the yolk mixture. If necessary, add a little rum to moisten the mixture. Gently fold in the egg whites. Turn into a buttered and floured baking pan and bake at 200°C for 50 minutes. Remove the cake from the pan immediately. When cool dust with confectioners' sugar mixed with cinnamon.

Sun in a Bottle

Capri is known for its quality citrus fruits, which grow in the many groves around the island. The pulp of the oranges, tangerines, and lemons is used to prepare delicious preserves; the rinds are used to prepare exquisite aromatic liqueurs. The peels of a fruit with a remarkably delicate flavor — the lemon, from strictly organic growers – with the addition of a few common ingredients like water, alcohol, and sugar, make the famous limoncello. This intensely-flavored, high-proof liqueur with its characteristic color seems to contain all the energy of the sun that shines in the eternally clear sky of the island. Production at the industrial level has permitted growers to enlarge their groves, all to the benefit of the local economy. But you can make your own, even far from Capri, following the recipe below.

Limoncello

| 1 quart, 190-proof grain alcohol | 4 cups (2 pounds) sugar |
| 1 quart water | 6 lemons |

Select very fresh, preferably unwaxed lemons; wipe with a damp cloth. Peel, taking care to remove only the yellow part of the rind, leaving the white inner rind on the fruit. Chop the peel very finely. Place in a large glass jar with the alcohol and allow to stand for 7 to 10 days.
Boil the water with the sugar for 5 minutes; allow the syrup to cool, then add to the jar with the lemon peel infusion. Allow to stand for one week, then filter the liquid and bottle for storage.

The Nectar of Capri

The providential combination of fertile soil that lends itself well to cultivation and a sea teeming with fish, since time immemorial primary sources of sustenance for the population of Capri, has given rise to traditions in food and wine among the finest to be found anywhere. The unadulterated, genuine flavors of the typical local dishes have always been accompanied – and above all enhanced – by the excellent wines of the island's vineyards. The vine growing and wine-making tradition of Capri goes far back in time, and has been lauded in the memoirs of such famous personalities as the German historian Ferdinand Gregorovius and the French writer Maxime Du Camp, both of whom visited Capri in the mid-1800's.
The many wineries founded during that century offer guided tours of the cellars and local wines for sale. On Capri, Bacchus' nectar has for about 20 years proudly borne the coveted D.O.C. (Denomination of Controlled Origin) mark. The white wine of this land is dry, light (11% alcohol), unmistakably tart, and excellent with antipastos and fish dishes. The red wine, so much appreciated by Du Camp, with its full, round flavor, slightly sugary and recalling the taste of strawberry, goes well with meat dishes.

USEFUL INFORMATION

GEOGRAPHICAL NOTES

The Island of Capri lies between 40°30'40"N and 40°16'48"N latitude and 14°11'54"E and 14°16'19"E longitude in the Gulf of Naples. The island's perimeter measures about 17 km, for a total area of 10.36 square kilometers; it is 6.17 km in length and varies in breadth between 2.7 and barely 1.2 km at its narrowest point. The island hosts two municipalities, Capri and Anacapri. The town of Capri, on the eastern side of the island, embraces Marina Grande — the port — to the north and Marina Piccola to the south. Anacapri, on the western slope of the island, is separated from Capri by Monte Solaro (589 m). The best seasons for visiting Capri are spring and fall, when the temperature is moderate.

Arriving on Capri

From Marina Grande, the "heart" of Capri can be reached in 10 minutes in one of the island's unique taxis or in only 5 minutes on the funicular. Taxis or buses will take you to Anacapri.
The territory of the Town of Capri is almost entirely closed to vehicle traffic. Remember that the hotels offer a paid porter service from the port.

☎ Code: 081-

PUBLIC SERVICES

Banks
Capri
Banca di Roma
Piazza Umberto I 19   tel. 081-8375942
Banca Popolare dell'Irpinia
Via Camerelle 25/27 tel. 081-8375250
Banco di Napoli
Via V. Emanuele 37/39   tel. 081-8376133
Credito Italiano
Via Roma 75 tel. 081-8370511
Monte dei Paschi di Siena
Via V. Emanuele 61   tel. 081-8389408
Marina Grande
Banco di Napoli
Via C. Colombo 78   tel. 081-8378005
Anacapri
Banco di Napoli
Via G. Orlandi 150 tel. 081-8371202
Monte dei Paschi di Siena
Via Caposcuro I tel. 081-8372193

Bureaux de Change
Capri
Ufficio Cambio
Via Roma 33 tel. 081-8370785
La Piazzetta
Piazza Umberto I 10
tel. 081-8370557
Anacapri
La Piazzetta 2
Piazza Vittoria 2b tel. 081-8373146

Carabinieri
Capri Via Prov.le Marina Grande 42
tel. 081-8370000
Anacapri Piazza San Nicola 16

tel. 081-8371011

City Hall – Municipio di Anacapri
Via Fenice I   tel. 081-8370271

City Hall – Municipio di Capri
Piazza Umberto I 9   tel. 081-8386111

Couriers and Shipping Agents
Capri
Capri Mail Service
Via Listrieri 2/A tel. 081-8376902
Emitrans
Via Prov.le Marina Grande 2
tel. 081-8370941
Esposito Trasporti
Via M. Serena 7/A tel. 081-8377335
Gambardella Service
Via Gradoni Sopramonte 7/A
tel. 081-8378830
PAD Trasporti
Via Prov. Anacapri 2   tel./fax 081-8378362
RIA Express
Piazza Umberto I tel. 081-8378932
Anacapri
Autotrasporti Belfiore
Via Nuova del Faro 61   tel. 081-8372095
Ca.Ma.Sca. Autotrasporti
Via Pagliaro 32 tel. 081-8372001

Customs Office
Marina Grande
Port waterfront — tel. 081-8376728

Customs Service-Guardia di Finanza
Capri
Via Sopramonte 6 tel. 081-8370604

Electricity Emergency Service
Capri tel. 081-8376260
Anacapri tel. 081-8371160

Fire Department
Capri — Via Prov. Marina Grande 37
tel. 081-8370222

Harbor Office
Marina Grande tel. 081-8370226

Hospital
Capri Azienda Sanitaria Locale Napoli 5
Via Prov. Anacapri 5 tel. 081-8381111

Emergency Medical Service
Via P.S. Cimino tel. 081-8381239
Emergency Room tel. 081-8381205

Left-Luggage Office
Capri: Via Acquaviva

Lost and Found
c/o Municipio di Capri
Piazza Umberto I tel. 081-8386111
c/o Municipio di Anacapri
Via Caprile 30 tel. 081-8372423
Municipal Police
Capri
Piazza Umberto I 9 tel. 081-8386203

Marina Grande
Piazza Vittoria tel. 081-8386223
Anacapri
Via Caprile 30 tel. 081-8372423

Pharmacies
Capri
Farmacia Internazionale
Via Roma 24 tel. 081-8370485
Farmacia Quisisana
Via le Botteghe 12 tel. 081-8370185
Marina Grande
Farmacia del Porto
Via C. Colombo 27 tel. 081-8375844
Anacapri
Farmacia Barile
Piazza Vittoria 28 tel. 081-8371460

Police
Capri
Via Roma 70 tel. 081-8374211

Porter Service
Capri
Piazza Martiri d'Ungheria 18
tel. 081-8370179

Port Workers' Cooperative
Via Prov. Marina Grande 270
tel. 081-8370896

Post and Telegraph Offices
Capri
Via Roma 50 tel. 081-8370215
Marina Grande
Via Prov. Marina Grande tel. 081-8377229
Anacapri
Viale De Tommaso tel. 081-8372168

Taxis and Funicular
Capri
S.I.P.P.I.C. SpA
Via Acquaviva 2 tel. 081-8370420
Upper Funicular Station   tel. 081-8370420
Staiano Autotrasporti
Via Marina Grande tel. 081-8370740
Anacapri
Staiano Autotrasporti
Via Filietto 13 tel. 081-8372422

Taxi Service Società Cooperativa Tassisti Capresi A.r.l.
Via Acquaviva 5 tel 081-8376657

Telephone and Fax Service
Capri
Piazza Umberto I tel. 081-8375550

Tourist Offices Azienda autonoma di soggiorno e turismo
Capri
P.tta I. Cerio tel. 081-8375308
Anacapri
Via G. Orlandi 19/a tel. 081-8371524

Azienda autonoma di soggiorno cura e turismo
Capri
Via P. Cimino tel. 081-8370424

93

Tourist Port
Consorzio PTC
Capri
Via Marina Grande 3 tel. 081-8374075

Tourist Port
Marina Grande
Via C. Colombo
tel. 081-8377602 / 081-8378950
fax 081-8375318

Tourist Transportation
Consorsio Noleggiatori
Capresi
Anacapri
Via Filetto 13 tel. 081-8372422

Tours of the Grotta
Azzurra
Gruppo Motoscafisti
di Capri
Via Marina Grande 59   tel. 081-8375646

Waterworks
Emergency Service
Capri Capri Multiservizi S.p.A.
tel. 081-8379646
Anacapri c/o Comune
tel. 081-8387111

Weather Center
Anacapri
Damecuta-Eliporto   tel. 081-8372750

FERRIES AND SHIPPING LINES

Remember that in the spring, summer, and autumn, non-residents are prohibited from using private cars, motorcycles, and motor-scooters.

Alilauro
Naples — Via F. Caracciolo   tel. 081-7611004
Capri — Marina Grande   tel. 081-8376995
Aliscafi SNAV
Naples — tel. 7612348   fax 7612141
Capri — Marina Grande   tel. 081-8377577
Caremar SpA
Naples — Molo Beverello
tel. 081-5513882/5805111   fax 081-5514551
Capri — Marina Grande tel. 081-8370700
NLG Navigazione Libera del Golfo
Naples — Molo Beverello
tel. 081-5527209   fax 081-5525589
Capri — Marina Grande   tel. 081-8370819

TOURS IN CAPRI
Certosa di San Giacomo
tel. 081-8370385
Tours daily from 9 am to 2 pm. Free admittance. Closed Mondays.
Chiesa di San Michele
Opening hours: April to October, 10 am to 6 pm; Sundays from 10 am to 2 pm.
Grotta Azzurra
Tours daily from 9 am to one hour before sunset. Motorboat from Marina Grande.
Centro Caprense I. Cerio — P.za I. Cerio

tel. 081-8370858
Imperial Villa
(Villa of Tiberius)
Opening hours (weekdays and holidays): 9 am to sunset.

TOURS IN ANACAPRI

Villa San Michele
Fondazione Axel Munthe
Via Capodimonte 34   tel. 081-8371401
Opening hours (weekdays and holidays): 9 am to sunset.

HOTELS IN CAPRI

*****

Hotel Quisisana
Via Camerelle 2
tel. 081-8370788

****

Hotel La Pazziella
P.za Giuliani 4
tel. 081-8370044
Hotel Calypso
Via I. Cerio
tel. 081-8370484 — fax 081-8370550
Hotel Casa Morgano
Via Tragara 6
tel. 081-8370158
Hotel La Palma
Via V. Emanuele 39
tel. 081-8370133
Hotel La Residenza
Via F.Serena 22
tel. 081-8370833
Hotel La Scalinatella
Via Tragara 8/10
tel. 081-8370633
Hotel Luna
Via G. Matteotti 3
tel. 081-8370433
Hotel Mamela
Via Campo di Teste 8
tel. 081-8375255
Hotel Palatium
Via Prov. Marina Grande
tel. 081-8376144
Hotel Punta Tragara
Via Tragara 57
tel. 081-8370844
Hotel Regina Cristina
Via F. Serena 20
tel. 081-8370744   fax 081-8370550
Hotel Semiramis
Via D. Biragho 4
tel. 081-8376129
Hotel Sirene
Via Camerelle 51
tel. 081-8370102
Hotel Villa Brunella
Via Tragara
tel. 081-8370122 — fax 081-8370430
Hotel Weber-Ambassador
Via Marina Piccola 188
tel. 081-8370141

***

Hotel Capri
Via Roma 71
tel. 081-8370003   fax 081-8378913
Hotel Esperia
Via Sopramonte 41
tel. 081-8370933
Hotel Gatto Bianco
Via V. Emanuele 32
tel. 081-8370203

Hotel La Canasta
Via Campo di Teste 6
tel. 081-8370561   fax 081-8376675
Hotel La Certosella
Via Tragara 13/15
tel. 081-8370713
Hotel La Floridiana
Via Campo di Teste 16
tel. 081-8370101
Hotel La Minerva
Via Occhio Marino 8
tel. 081-8375221
Hotel La Vega
Via Occhio Marino 10
tel. 081-8370881   fax 081-8370342
Hotel Nautilus
Via Marina Piccola 98
tel. 081-8375322
Hotel San Felice
Via Li Campi 13
tel. 081-8376122
Hotel Villa Certosa
Via I. Cerio 10
tel. 081-8376000
Hotel Villa Sarah
Via Tiberio
tel. 081-8377817

**

Aida
Via D.Birago 18
tel. 081-8370366
Hotel Belsito
Via Matermània 11
tel. 081-8370969
Hotel Belvedere e Tre Re
Via Marina Grande 138
tel. 081-8370345
Hotel Florida
Via Fuorlovado 34
tel. 081-8370042
Hotel Italia
Via Marina Grande
tel. 081-8370262
Hotel La Reginella
Via Matermània 36
tel. 081-8376829
Hotel Villa Krupp
Via Matteotti
tel. 081-8370362
Hotel Villa Pina
Via Tuoro 11
tel. 081-8377517

*

ABC
Via Roma   tel. 081-8370683
Da Giorgio
Via Roma 34   tel. 081-8375777
Guarracino
Via Mulo 13   tel. 081-8377140
La Prora
Via Castello 6   tel. 081-8370281
La Tosca
Via D. Birago 5   tel. 081-8370989
Quattro Stagioni
Via Marina Piccola   tel. 081-8370041
Stella Maris
Via Roma 27   tel. 081-8370452
Villa Palomba
Via Mulo 3   tel. 081-8377322

RESTAURANTS IN CAPRI

'A Cianciola
Via Acquaviva 20   tel. 081-8370282
Ai Faraglioni
Via Camerelle 75   tel. 081-8370320
Al Campanile

Via Roma 2 tel. 081-8377370
Al Grottino
Via Longano 27 tel. 081-8370584
Albys
Via Mulo 4 tel. 081-8377223
Aurora
Via Fuorlovado 18 tel. 081-8370181
Bagni di Gioia
Marina Piccola beach tel. 081-8377702
Bagni Smeraldo
Via Marina Grande 12 tel. 081-8377212
Bagni Tiberio
Via Palazzo a Mare tel. 081-8377688
Belsito
Via Matermania 8 tel. 081-8378750
Biberius
Vico Sella Orta 10 tel. 081-8370431
Bocciodromo
Trav. lo Palazzo 2 tel. 081-8377414
Buca di Bacco da Serafina
Via Longano 25 tel. 081-8370723
Buonocore
Via V. Emanuele 35 tel. 081-8377826
Capri Moon
Marina Grande 86/a tel. 081-8377953
Capri
Via Roma 71
tel. 081-8370003 / 081-8375207
Casanova
Via le Botteghe 46 tel. 081-8377642
Ciro a Mare
Via Marina Piccola tel. 081-8370264
Da Francesco
Largo Fontana tel. 081-8376490
Da Gemma
Via Madre Serafina 6
tel. 081-8370461 / 081-8377113
Da Gioia
Beachfront at Marina Piccola
tel. 081-8377702
Da Giorgio
Via Roma 34
tel. 081-8370898 / 081-8375777
Da Luigi ai Faraglioni
Via Faraglioni tel. 081-8370591
Da Maria
Via Marina Piccola tel. 081-8375648
Da Paolino
Via Palazzo a Mare 11 tel. 081-8375611
Da Tonino
Via Dentecala 12 tel. 081-8376718
Europa
Marina Grande 4 tel. 081-8370344
Gallo D'Oro
Via C. Colombo 21 tel. 081-8370853
Il Tinello
Via l'Abate 1/3 tel. 081-8377673
Il Verginiello
Via Palazzo 25 tel. 081-8370944
Isidoro
Via Roma 19 tel. 081-8377252
L'Approdo
Piazza Ferraro 7 tel. 081-8378990
La Cantinella
Via G. Matteotti 8 tel. 081-8370616
La Canzone del Mare
Via Marina Piccola 93 tel. 081-8370104
La Capannina
Via le Botteghe 12/14 tel. 081-8370732
La Certosella
Via Tragara 13/15
tel. 081-8370713 / 081-8370722
La Cisterna
Via Madre Serafina 5

tel. 081-8375620
La Colombaia
Via Camerelle 2 tel. 081-8370788
La Floridiana
Via Campo di Teste 16
tel. 081-8370166 / 081-8370434
La Fontelina
loc. Faraglioni tel. 081-8370845
La Palette
Via Matermània 36 tel. 081-8370500
La Piazzetta
Via Marina Piccola tel. 081-8377827
La Pigna
Via Roma 8 tel. 081-8370280
La Savardina
Via Lo Capo 8 tel. 081-8376300
La Scogliera
Via Prov. Marina Grande
tel. 081-8376144
La Terrazza
Via Camerelle 85 tel. 081-8376596
Le Grottelle
Via Matermània 3 tel. 081-8375719
Le Ondine
Via M. Grande tel. 081-8375453
Le Sirene
Via Marina Piccola tel. 081-8370221
Longano
Via Longano 9 tel. 081-8370187
Luna Caprese
Via Tiberio 7 tel. 081-8376503
Medj Pub
Via M. C. Serena tel. 081-8375148
Moscardino
Via Roma 28 tel. 081-8370687
Onda D'Oro
Via Marina Piccola 122 tel. 081-8370698
Quo Vadis Pub
Via P. S. Cimino 10
Ristorante Relais
Via V. Emanuele 39 tel. 081-8370133
San Costanzo
Via Marucella 26 tel. 081-8377947
Serena
Via V. Emanuele 19 tel. 081-8370966
Settanni
Via Longano 5 tel. 081-8370105
Sollievo
Via Fuorlovado 36 tel. 081-8370665
Torre Saracena
Via Krupp 1 tel. 081-8370646
Villa Verde Vico Sella Orta 6a
tel. 081-8377024

HOTELS IN ANACAPRI

****

Hotel Capri Palace S.p.A.
Via Capodimonte 2/B
tel. 081-8373800
Hotel Europa Palace
Viale Axel Munthe
tel. 081-8373800 fax 081-8373191

***

Hotel Caesar Augustus
Via G. Orlandi 4
tel. 081-8371421
Hotel Il Girasole
Via La Guardia 1 tel. 081-8372351
Hotel San Michele
Via G. Orlandi 1/3 tel. 081-8371427

**

Hotel Bellavista
Via G. Orlandi 10 tel. 081-8371463
Hotel Biancamaria
Via G. Orlandi 54 tel. 081-8371000
Hotel Carmencita
Viale De Tommaso 6/A
Hotel Loreley
Via G. Orlandi 12/a tel. 081-8371440

*

Villa Eva
Via Grotta Azzurra 8 tel. 081-8371549

RESTAURANTS IN ANACAPRI

'A Curtiglia
Via Nuova del Faro 86 tel. 081-8373334
Add'o Riccio
Via Grotta Azzurra tel. 081-8371380
Al Nido d'Oro
Via G. Orlandi 295 tel. 081-8371223
Aumm Aumm
Via Caprile 18 tel. 081-8372061
Barbarossa
Via Porta 1 tel. 081-8371483
La Giara
Via G. Orlandi 67 tel. 081-8373860
Le Arcate
Viale De Tommaso 24 tel. 081-8373325
Lido del Faro
Loc. Punta Carena tel. 081-8371798
Viale De Tommaso 32 tel. 081-8372148
Island Pub
Viale De Tommaso 6 tel. 081-8373641
Cristal
Via Capodimonte 11 tel. 081-837 302
Da Gelsomina
Via Migliera 72 tel. 081-8371499
Eden Paradiso
Via G. Orlandi tel. 081-8371583
Toll-free 167-015651
Europa Palace
Via Capodimonte tel. 081-8373800
Grottino
Via G. Orlandi 21 tel. 081-8371066
Il Cucciolo
Nuova Trav. Veterino 50 tel. 081-8371917
Il Ristoro
Via Caprile 1 tel. 081-8373671
Il Saraceno
Via Trieste e Trento 18 tel. 081-8372099
Il Solitario
Via G. Orlandi 96 tel. 081-8371382
La Giara
Via G. Orlandi 67 tel. 081-8373860
La Rondinella
Via G. Orlandi 295 tel. 081-8371223
La Vedette
Via S. Michele 11 tel. 081-8371548
Le Arcate
Viale De Tommaso 24 tel. 081-8373325
Lido del Faro
loc. Punta Carena tel. 081-8371798
Mamma Giovanna
Via Boffe 3/5 tel. 081-8372057
Materita
Via G. Orlandi 140 tel. 081-8373375
Vittoria
Piazza Vittoria 1 tel. 081-8371464

CONTENTS